CW00504824

# POSITIVE THINKING

## Be An Optimist And Change Your Life

SOPHIE SYEAR

# Sommario

# INTRODUCTION

Psychologists often say that it is up to us to feel good or bad. This statement isn't without its controversy, as there are those who think there are circumstances that don't depend on us and may make us feel bad.

It is true that many external experiences outside of us can cause our moods to wobble. But it is also true that our mind processes every event, and the meaning we will give will not depend on anyone, but solely on ourselves.

Positive thinking is closely associated with optimism. A person who positively perceives the world and sees the "good side of things" will feel better mental and physical health than a person who thinks in a negative, anxious, even depressed manner.

A positive thought is not a new concept. It is an autosuggestion-based therapeutic approach that seeks to adhere to the topic to positive ideas. The person should have access to well-being and achieve optimal health by repeating positive messages twenty times a day.

Thinking on the body can act directly. You feel good when you replace negative thoughts with calm, confidence, and peace. Additionally, in overcoming sleep disorders, muscle tension, anxiety, and fatigue, positive thinking can help. People who think negatively are suffering more from anxiety and depression.

Positive thinking has a positive effect on healthy and sick people's survival. Having a good morality, however, also predisposes to behave more "positive" in health terms. Indeed, studies show that more virtuous behaviors accompany this disposition of mind. Of course, just because of tension, our feelings, or our thoughts, we don't get sick. But we can now assume that our emotions and actions cause many of the symptoms and diseases.

The thoughts are powerful. Our lives have always been shaped by them. Think positively, and look forward to positive results. Situations and circumstances will, therefore, change!

# CHAPTER ONE

## The Power of Positive Thinking

"With time, everyone finds their place." Some call it God, others Allah or Jehovah, and still others "Karma," that mysterious entity that never judges. Everyone believes what his morals, his culture or his religion dictate to him.

But can we trust this statement? Is our destiny really written? It is difficult to answer this question clearly. In any case, each of us is unique, and our actions can be "good or bad."

When we go through difficult passes, if we want to get out of it, we have to try to outdo ourselves, to know ourselves better, and to take advantage of crises that we can experience in our lives.

Finally, we realize that our happiness is stronger than anything and that nothing and nobody will be able to reach it. This is how we can "find our place in life" and take a new path.

**Always go-ahead**

Many of you are wondering how it is possible to

make every moment of life wonderful. Obviously, there is no magic formula, and the method we propose is not infallible.

Whatever we do, we will always have to face events that come before us against our will. However, that does not mean that we deserve these events, or that they happen to us because we are a fundamentally bad person.

You just have to overcome these events so that you can grow as a person and become emotionally stronger. If you apply this method, you will certainly know better days.

By having positive thoughts, you reduce the risk of having to deal with negative events. In fact, positive thinking is a very powerful weapon, and many people do not know about it. If you manage to master it, you will be surprised at the results.

To get there, every time a negative event comes your way, you must try to find a solution quickly and see the positive side of things. This way, you will gain self-esteem and self-confidence because you will have managed to get by on your own.

You will consider yourself as a strong, active person, and able to overcome any kind of obstacle. In fact, positivity calls for positivity!

**You reap what you sow**

One of the ways to master the "power" of positive thinking is altruism. In fact, if we listen to our loved ones when they need to confide in us and try to help them solve their problems, then we will feel more in harmony with ourselves.

We will gain a lot of self-esteem thanks to this altruism that will make us a better person. If you help a friend, this one will definitely make it to you when it's your turn to need support. In the end, everyone is a winner!

If, on the contrary, we cultivate negative thought, then it will only have the effect of attracting even more negativity. There is no point in lying in bed and mourning and falling into self-compassion at the slightest annoyance.

# CHAPTER TWO

## How to turn a negative thought into positive thinking?

Can negative thinking be transformed into positive thinking? Barbara Fredrickson, a psychologist at the University of North Carolina (USA), demonstrated how an optimistic attitude towards life could help the brain fight negative emotions. The researcher found that through certain exercises, the body can be trained to develop positive responses and multiply them, thereby generating a natural damper against stress and depression.

The first thing we have to make clear is that the thoughts we "declare war" will attack us. If we resist, oppose, or deny negative thinking whenever it comes to our mind, it will persist and remain in our minds. Each thought will trigger more thoughts of its own nature until it generates a whole cognitive flood that does not help us.

The thoughts we have can affect our daily lives and even our emotions and behaviors. It is important to understand the relationship between counteracting negative thinking and reducing its negative consequences. To do this, the first thing to do is to identify our automatic negative thinking patterns, which, by force of habit, have become part of our core beliefs.

Our fundamental beliefs are full of cognitive inclinations or distortions. It is time to identify and combat these distortions to generate positive thoughts in the face of each new situation. These inclinations or distortions make our mind eliminate information that does not suit us to maintain our beliefs and expand or increase the information that matches our way of living life.

*"The work of thinking resembles drilling a well: the water is cloudy at first, but soon becomes clearer."*
*-Chinese proverb-*

**Thoughts are just a modifiable part of you.**

The brain does not seek the truth, but to survive. In a prehistoric world, this form of mental behavior was very appropriate, but many things have changed today. There is now less need to respond quickly to survive, as an appropriate response to each situation. We must remember that our brain can sometimes be mistaken: it can show us the situation as it thinks it is, not as it really is.

The mind tries to save energy, to quickly provide us with a concrete answer to try to take control and offer us security and tranquility. It is in these mental shortcuts that the greatest distortions occur. Our primitive brain tends to act quickly, in the same way, which our ancestors survive, and that is why we face an excess of generalizations, negative filtrations, and mental rigidity when we manage information at full speed.

Today, in our society, there are very few real danger situations in which we find ourselves in everyday life; Almost all threat situations are imagined or whose consequences are exaggerated. Processing information quickly makes us fall into prejudices that try to sharpen a distorted image by how quickly we try to process it.

One of the biggest involuntary distortions is to accept as absolute truth the probability that something might happen. This causes us to act anxiously or depressed without the fact. Only about 20% of our thoughts actually happen. So our thoughts should not be the judges of our lives, but the spectators.

*"Not even your worst enemy can do as much damage as your own thoughts."*

## Understand your mind and your mind will understand it.

For the majority of us, we have the habit of devoting some of our attention to the activities we are doing right now, while the mind and thoughts are focused on other issues. To act in this way is to live with "automatic piloting", taking care of what we do without being aware of the details of the moment.

Being fully aware of what is happening here and

now is the ideal state to combat negative thoughts. Accepting that such thinking is necessary under certain circumstances, and a vicious circle of nourishing negative premonitions provides us with the key to replacing them with more reality-adjusted thoughts.

There may be elements of certain situations that we cannot change, such as pain, illness, or a difficult circumstance, but at least we realize how we can respond or respond to whatever happens to us. In doing so, we will be able to develop strategies for changing the relationship we have with our circumstances and the filters - not always friends - we use to process them.

*"The hunter chasing two rabbits doesn't catch either."*

# CHAPTER THREE

## Negative thoughts: unhealthy habits to hunt.

The negative thoughts take an important place in our minds so that they can prevent the point we literally live. You may aspire to a new life but your thoughts are your first obstacle.

I would like to talk about 10 negative thoughts that come up most often in our minds in order to be aware of them to improve them and turn them into mental strength.

## 1. Have a bad self-image.

Many of us may have a bad image of ourselves because we do not trust ourselves, we focus on the negative; ruminate on failures and difficulties instead of seeing the opportunities and learning that we have learned. Of our past mistakes.

It is important to understand that the more energy I concentrate in one direction, the more I will go in that direction that I visualize in my mind.

Everything happens above all in our heads. By imagining our mind as a box that we do not stop to fill negative thoughts, you realize that there is more room to put positive thoughts and build good self-esteem.

For example, by taking the habit of writing down everything that we have done well during the day, we are obliged to focus our energy on the good things and not dwell on the bad things that bring us nothing.

We have inside ourselves the spotlight of our life. If our mental state is unclear, it is certain that our life outside as we live it will not flourish because it will reflect our inner state.

On the other hand, if you have a lucid and clear mind, everything will be aligned in your life to go in the direction you want: to build a family, find the job of your life, start a business, go around the world, learn a new language, communicate your knowledge and skills on a large scale,

A clear and lucid mind is synonymous with power. Power is our ability to believe in ourselves and associate a positive image of ourselves. Once the mind is clear, outside actions can follow to go in the direction of your choice.

When doing actions, do not try to ask if they are good or bad. You will always find fault with what you are doing because we often idealize things in our heads. But the key is to always give the best of yourself to not blame yourself.


## 2. The look of others and the need for approval.

Another thought that is important to work on is always asking yourself what others think about us. We do not care what people think of us.

How many people live through the eyes of others for years to see dozens of years and finally realize that they lived the life of another or in the place of another: his parents, his teachers, his colleagues, television, ...

How many people have everything to be happy: husband / wife, child (ren), good salary, nice house, etc. but who basically do not feel happy, who find that the weeks are long, who wait for the weekend with impatience and even who sometimes have difficulty to appreciate the moments spent with family.

How many people feel completely desiccated from within because they do not live what they are made of?

Always wondering what others think of us is synonymous with paralysis. We paralyze ourselves to live our right to be free, to be oneself because our fear of the eyes of others forces us to play a role, a character that we are not at the bottom.

We over-stimulate our left brain to try to anticipate, understand and explain what others will think of us at each of our actions. If I do that, he'll think about it and the other will think maybe that about me. We diminish ourselves first in our heads before even trying to express our true selves.

That's why you do not ever miss an opportunity that can make you happy by being yourself even if this opportunity does not please others.


### 3. Regret the past.
Another negative thought to forget is the regret

about our past memories. In life, we sometimes have to make certain choices that force us to make decisions.

Depending on the choices we make, we refuse to do anything new, to try the experience of his life, go on an adventure, tell him "I love you", start an activity out of fear or by excessive security needs that paralyze us once again. Fear is our worst counselor.

This fear or need for security traps us in a comfort zone that destroys us slowly without realizing it. By choosing our comfort zone and refusing the change that is inevitable, we condemn ourselves to regret the events of the past. To avoid regret, plan 10 years later and say this: "We rarely regret having dared, but still not to have tried."

Life is too short to live in regret for our past memories of what we should have done or not done. If we did it, it was because there was a reason. If we do not understand at the moment, it is that there was an apprenticeship to acquire, a passage to live to allow us to go where we want.

We are sometimes forced to live the worst to get the

best so useless to waste time to regret it. Only those who do not do anything ever happen to them.

That's why let's stop fixing our eyes on the past that we cannot change but turn them in front of us to what we want and the result we want. The path will be traced as and when.


## 4. Project yourself in the future.

Unlike the past, we have another habit of negative thinking that is constantly projecting into the future. What will be the future? How are things going to happen if I do this if I do that?

So lost in the whirlwind of our thoughts absorbed by our left brain that we prevent ourselves from living the present moment. The present moment is lived through the action.

If you are in action, you are in the moment and you stop thinking. When you think, the action is stopped, the present nonexistent and you live in your past or in your future.

It is important to think and take a step back from our actions but it is even more important to find a balance and to distinguish between our useful and constructive thoughts to move forward in life and the whirlwind of thought that prevents us from living. It's very different.

Planning your day of the day before the night before bed is a very good way of thinking, visualize your dreams that you want to achieve is a good way of thinking also; it enriches us and pushes us to take action. The thought is constructive and benevolent.

On the other hand, if one thinks too much, for example, of all the possible scenarios that could occur to do such and such a thing, one becomes a prisoner of one's mind and one prevents oneself from taking action.

The whirlwind of thought raises our fears and our doubts that paralyze us. The thought is malicious and destructive of any perspective of evolution.

## 5. Self-criticism.

Self-criticism is different from questioning. Questioning is an interrogation of one's current position to try to clarify one's vision because it is known as mental clarity = power.

On the other hand, self-criticism is the way in which one takes a step back to criticize oneself but that will not, in any case, make progress. On the contrary, it is the best way to have a bad image of oneself as we have seen previously.

Self-criticism is acting on oneself a bit like an incomprehensible and authoritarian dictator, parent or teacher who never tolerates error. By doing so, we literally "kill" the student who is in us and in constant pursuit of learning.

The thirst for knowledge is something human because associated with curiosity; it is one of the energizing actions that one can achieve. Being curious about everything is one of the best ways to give back energy and to feel alive.

Let us leave the time to learn, to learn from our mistakes, to learn from our lived experiences to move serenely in life. It's very simple, every time we do something, an action is asked, and there are two possible outcomes:

- Either I won and I take a step closer to my

goal,

- Either I learned or I know that I have to change something in my next action.

In any case, I know that I do not lose because I am in permanent and continuous learning. I do not know anyone who knows everything about everything; it's humanly impossible, so let's give this right to the error and stop being harsh and rigid with ourselves.

This does not mean to let oneself be carried away without ambition or purpose in life because sooner or later, one will not feel as dry as if one were living through other looks as said before. But self-criticism by focusing on our mistakes and failures is the best way to burn oneself.

## 6. To lie to oneself.

Too often, we hide behind the lie to avoid the pain and feeling of uneasiness that an uncomfortable situation can cause.

To avoid these moments of stress and difficult emotional pressure that we are sometimes caught off guard, the brain constantly seeks ease and the reptilian brain, particularly driven by the survival instinct will seek to find the comfort zone at most. quick.

Thus, it is very easy to make a lie because it makes the situation comfortable and soothing right now. In the long run, that's another story.

When we start to lie to others, we lie to ourselves because we do not assume to be the real person we are, that is to say, that we play a character to "caress" the other in the direction of the hair.

We put a barrier between ourselves and the character we play by a lie. It is important to understand that only the truth can destroy this ephemeral character that has been created to protect itself for a moment.

Sooner or later, you will have to be truthful because the fictional character that is created to please everyone will take up so much of our life, lying after lies that we will own and make ourselves sick.

Sick physically or mentally, it does not matter, the accumulation of lies against oneself will have to come out in one way or another:

- Either by an open and confident expression of your personal truth by assuming yourself,
- Or by a disease that the physical or mental body cannot cash.

Even if the truth is sometimes hard to express, to swallow and to admit for your interlocutor, it is important to be true. Better a true person who can hurt, a wrong person who caresses you in the direction of the hair and makes you waste your time while you realize his lie.

## 7. Focus on what you do not want.

Many people know what they do not want but very few know what they want. It is a very disturbing thought and mental habit because focusing one's energy and attention on what one does not want is going to point us precisely in that direction. Remember, we are going there; we focus our energy and our attention.

If you keep thinking, for example, that you do not want your girlfriend to leave you or that this type of thinking is taking up more and more space in your mind, you can be sure that this energy that you are directing will affect your mental state. the meaning of the thought.

If your mental state goes in that direction, the lightness decreases and the projector inside of us will change the point of observation. Thus, the situation outside will inevitably change as you have changed yourself inside. Everything starts first of all in our heads. Action follows our mental state to be realized in a matter outside.

That's why let's stop focusing on what we do not want but rather on what we want. If you do not know what you want, you must first start there otherwise your mental clarity will not be optimal.

Finally, take everything you do not want and deduce the opposite in your head, it may give you ideas to know what you want.

## 8. Compare yourself to others.

We have always been used to competing with others. At school, at sports and sometimes even in families. This feeling of competition is very destabilizing because it pushes us to see each other as a danger and someone to flee or reject.

To see others as a threat or a danger to avoid is the best way to find oneself alone and to shut oneself in one's world without wanting to express it and expose it to the world.

I'm not saying that you should not be competitive or compare yourself, but do it in a way that makes sense for you. It is important to understand that there will always be better and worse than us in all areas of our lives.

There will always be better than us, which is why comparing ourselves to others is the best way to get discouraged, to sabotage our will to go further and make ourselves unhappy. On the other hand, we can compare ourselves to ourselves and the approach is thus completely different.

So we progress gradually at its own pace by looking at our individual performances and only ours, not those of others. The others have their assets and their gifts that life has given them. You have yours.

Use them. The need to fulfill oneself and to surpass oneself is done in this way and not by comparing oneself with others.

That's why you do not try to be better than others but to be better than the person you were yesterday or a year ago.


### 9. Make yourself feel guilty.

Guilt is also a negative thought that burns our wings. Indeed, when we let our real person act, we act for his good, live his right to be free and we can sometimes feel guilty to do so.

Guilty of being selfish, guilty of having failed something, guilty of hurting someone. We live in this feeling that we do not have the right to make mistakes and that we must be extremely generous to the point of forgetting ourselves.

It is important to understand that if you do not think a minimum to take care of yourself for example, no one will do it for you. Not because others are selfish but because they have their business to handle.

In addition, it is not the responsibility of others to manage your business, it's up to you. That's why do not be afraid to think a little about yourself to grow and grow.

How do you want to help someone and pull him up if you have not taken the time to raise yourself and others to your height? Guilt is a feeling that sometimes gnaws at us and prevents us from fully expressing our full potential.

Let us accept ourselves as we are, accept our mistakes no matter how big, there is always an apprenticeship behind us. Sometimes our biggest dreams are disguised by our worst nightmares.

The errors, the failures are obligatory passages to live the sought-after happiness that is why we have in no case need of guilt to diminish us and sink in the self-criticism.


## 10. Impatience.

Last negative thought of which I would like to speak, those are those relating to our state of impatience. We got used to having everything, immediately at the moment.

No doubt the new instantaneous communication technologies are partly responsible for this habit of thinking like that, that you have to have everything now.

It is clear that when something is done, it will take more or less time for the seed that has been planted to germinate.

Sometimes it will take 1 day, 1 week, 1 month, 1 year, 10 years, it will take the time it takes for it to germinate. Our universe is governed by a law that is called a law of cause and effect, that is to say, that each cause will have effects in the more or less long term and that each effect has necessarily a cause which is at the origin.

All this to say that when you plant a seed: find the man or woman of your life, find the work of your dreams, learn a new language, go around the world, etc. it will take more or less time. Give yourself time to learn how to water this seed that you have planted by your actions filled with good intentions.

Things are not instantly instantaneous as you can communicate with a friend or relative who is on the other side of the world.

When you feel impatience rising in you with all the doubts and fears that they let go with it, remember all the way you've traveled, the things you've learned, the obstacles you've overcome so far and that the essential is not the result but the direction to go.

A direction is an infinite path to evolution and self-knowledge while a result is a path in which one has drawn one's own limit that distorts our perception of happiness.

It is not by reaching the result so much hoped that one would be happy, on the contrary. Once reached, the feeling of fullness will be short-lived if the perspective of evolution is not redefined.

On the other hand, when one goes down a path and one knows that one is on the right track, it will take the time that it will take that the seeds that one put in the ground can germinate.

# Negative feelings: How to express them in a positive way?

Many people hide their negative feelings, driven by low self-esteem or ego. Others expect others to guess what they feel. Learn to express your feelings fearlessly and effectively.

No matter if you are excited, frustrated or sad, express your feelings the way that feels most comfortable. You may feel concerned about the conflicts that these feelings can generate with people close to you, but still worth expressing them. The following tips will help you put out your negative emotions and feelings without fear.

## 1. Think exactly how you feel

When you can define how you feel in one or two words, ambiguity lags and you can express your feelings, emotions and thoughts freely. Try to be careful because some people may misunderstand these emotions. The next step is to understand the level of your feelings, that is, how much anger or sadness you feel.

## 2. Identify the cause of your emotions.

Identify the reason or pretext behind your emotions. Maybe you just got fired from your job, for example. Once you have an apparent reason why you are affecting your life, you can view the situation objectively and reduce misunderstandings. Know the things that bother you and focus on them as you try to express them in words.

## 3. Express yourself by painting or writing.

There is no need to become the new Shakespeare, but you can express your feelings through journal entries, stories, or poems that talk about your emotions. You can also draw and focus on showing what you have in mind. Of course, this is something abstract, but don't worry because it's just about expressing yourself freely.

## 4. Get rid of anger with exercise

Anger is one of the most negative emotions for our

bodies and our mind. To avoid many of its negative effects, we can focus on having a good exercise session to break free. Find a physical activity that you can't hurt anyone but helps you get rid of anger easily. You can opt for kickboxing, running or some sport like volleyball or tennis.

## 5. Talk to someone you trust

Find someone you can trust to talk about your feelings. If you don't feel like talking directly, you can use a letter or email. This way you will get rid of your emotions and get answers that help you see the situation from another perspective.

## 6. Scream or cry... or both

Crying is a way of releasing emotions and can be very helpful in getting rid of what hurts you. Some people have difficulty crying even though they have to. If this is your case, you might see a sad movie that makes it easy for you to get in touch with your emotions.

## CHAPTER FOUR

## Self-esteem - reliable techniques for confidence

In short, self-esteem is your general opinion about yourself and your skills.

It can be high, low or on a scale somewhere in between. While everyone sometimes has doubts about themselves, low self-esteem (low self-esteem) can make you feel insecure, you will not be motivated and you will doubt your competences.

Fortunately, there are plenty of proven techniques that you can use to improve your self-esteem.

## What is self-assessment?

Self-esteem is an attitude toward oneself. Attitudes

generally contain three components:

- Behavioral (how we behave towards an object of attitude, in this case towards ourselves)
- Affective (what we feel about the object of attitude, i.e. here towards ourselves)
- Cognitive (what we think about the object of attitude - about ourselves)

Like all attitudes, self-esteem can also be divided into:

- public (of which we are aware and we can, for example, tell about it)
- hidden (whose origin we do not know)

Explicit self-assessment is a general belief in one's worth (for example, the ability to list one's advantages).

On the other hand, hidden self-assessment is the assessment of objects that we associate with each other. For this reason, it is shakier, because at different times we can take into account various purposes related to your "I". Hidden self-assessment will depend on this object.

Examples: hidden self-esteem increases after the victory of a sports team that we identify with, and decreases when we see something that reminds us of our problems - for example, we look at pictures of retouched models, which reduces self-esteem by associating with, e.g. overweight.

Sometimes self-esteem is treated in psychology as a trait - then we say that self-esteem is a permanent tendency to self- estimate positively or negatively.

The features are characterized by the fact that they are relatively constant throughout life (or because in psychology there is nothing "for sure" that "will never change in the slightest," but slow minor changes are of course possible).

The way we understand and define self-esteem depends on the psychological concept in which we consider it.

Generally speaking, people have positive self-esteem (both explicit and implicit) rather.

It should be noted that although high self-esteem means self-esteem, low self-esteem does not mean that we consider ourselves worthless - it instead means that we are not sure of our value and our self-esteem is shaky.

## What affects the level of our self-esteem?

### genes

The first "germination" of our self-esteem is independent of us - research shows that a huge part of the level of self-esteem is due to genetic inheritance. So self-confidence is a lot more about who we are (and how we were born) than about how many impressive successes we achieve in life.

### Personality traits

Another very important factor in the formation of self-esteem is innate personality traits - especially neuroticism, extraversion and conscientiousness.

These are three of the five so-called personality factors described in the Big Five theory by P. Costa and R. McRae. According to researchers, we can examine and describe each person's personality in five dimensions:

- Neuroticism: emotional stability: describes emotional balance, tendency to experience negative emotions and stress
- Extraversion - introversion: refers to the quantity and quality of experiencing interaction with other people
- Openness to experience: describes tolerance to emerging news and innate curiosity
- Agreeableness - antagonism: this is simply a type of attitude towards others (as more positive and favorable or negative)
- Conscientiousness - unfocused: describes the degree to which a person is organized, disciplined and persistent in activities that are to lead to a designated goal.

According to the Big Five theory, the features resulting from the above factors are universal and biologically conditioned. Robin's research shows that an increase in self-esteem is influenced by:

- high extraversion
- low neuroticism

- high diligence

## Life experience

The third factor, which we often intuitively list as the most important (or even the only) are the results of actions taken. Of course, the better results we achieve, the higher the self-esteem will be.

The most important are the situations confirming someone's agency - that is, how someone comes out of what depends on him (the most famous examples will be grades for learning or results at work).

## Learning from others

For our self-esteem, it is also indifferent to how other people perceive us. Of course, the most important will be the opinions of our loved ones, whom we believe count - a partner, family, friends, boss or colleagues.

Thus, we make our opinion similar to the idea of our loved ones about us - parents have a massive impact on shaping self-esteem (children will think similarly about themselves, as parents feel about them).

## How do we protect our self-esteem?

Because we intuitively feel that high self-esteem brings many benefits (and is just pleasant), we want to think about ourselves well. We may notice a number of actions (usually unconscious) that we do to increase our self-esteem or protect it against lowering in an emergency.

### We talk about ourselves well

To illustrate that people generally have a high tendency to rate themselves highly, an example of a better-than-average effect will be ideal. This effect appears when people are asked to rate themselves compared to others, to "most people".

Then it turns out that most people assess themselves as better drivers than most, more friendly people and with an above-average sense of humor. Of course, there is a paradox where - most people can't be better than most people.

Interestingly, lecturers are masters in this field - as many as 94% of them (according to Cross's research) consider themselves gifted with above-average ability to transfer knowledge to students.

## We explain it so that good light falls on us

These activities are very often called simply "excuses". Very often it is about looking outside for the cause of failure (for example I did not pass the exam because the questions were biased, not because I did not study).

We can explain each achieved result in any field in many ways. They can be:

- Global (more general) or specific (more detailed)
- Permanent (difficult to change quickly) or variable (temporary causes)
- Internal (resulting from ourselves) or external (resulting from our environment)

These options give us the opportunity to explain the situation in eight different ways.

Take, for example, the explanation of no promotion at work.

- Global, permanent and internal explanation: I'm too stupid
- Specific, variable and external explanation: the boss stood up with his left leg

Explaining internal causes increases emotional reactions (we feel more responsible).

Permanent causes, more than variables, influence our expectations for the future (failure explained by a permanent cause will influence the expectation of a similar failure in the future).

The global cause, however, affects the scope of our expectations in the future (global causes will extend to more areas).

For our self-esteem and well-being, a pessimistic explanation, i.e. searching for global, permanent and internal causes, is the most harmful. It may even be a risk factor for depression in the long run.

His opposite is attributive egotism, i.e. a situation in which we explain successes more internally and failures rather externally.

**We glory in someone else's glory.**

Floating in someone else's glory (also called "reflected light shining") involves taking part in positive effects and feeling positive emotions after someone else's success.

A perfect example is a study by Robert Cialdini and his team. The behavior of students of a particular university was examined depending on the success or failure of the university's football team.

It was observed more frequent putting on university shirts and the first person plural expression ("we won") after a successful match. However, after the match ended in defeat, no such behavior was noticed, and even the opposite narrative was seen ("they lost").

The effect of swimming in someone else's glory is the stronger, the more successful this person or group of people in whose glory we have to swim, and the stronger the closer we are to this person or group of people.

So, for example, we will feel the positive effects of the fact that our sister received a prestigious award than if it were a distant cousin.

## We move away from successful people in our field

Despite the phenomenon from the third point, successes may threaten our assessment, instead of increasing it. This happens when other people's successes related to a field that is important to us (because we start comparing our results with the results of a given person, and when that person achieves better results, there is a serious threat to our self-esteem).

In this situation, we basically have two simple ways to protect our self-esteem: we can either move away from the person or try to reduce the value of the field.

If closeness is threatening, because the other person is successful in the field in which we would like to achieve impressive results ourselves, the way to avoid adverse comparisons will be the loss of closeness.

Researcher Tesser has shown in his research that even siblings are particularly close to each other when each of them is involved and succeeds in different areas (for example, one achieves sports successes and the other scientific or artistic). If a brother or sister is involved in the same field, the emotional closeness felt between them decreases.

## We are changing the field in which we have been overcome

If it happens that a loved one achieves better results than ours , it is better (for our self-esteem) that this field becomes less important to us - because then the successes of this person will not only stop threats to our self-esteem but will even increase it thanks to " playing in someone else's glory "(see point three).

However, when it is the other way round, when our

results are higher in a given field than the results of people close to us - then it is better to think about the given field as very important, thanks to which our self-esteem and closeness with a given person will be maintained.

**affirm**

Affirmations are sentences that we "talk to each other" to convince ourselves about ourselves.

By means of what we say to ourselves, we try to convince ourselves of the value of ourselves as a good person, internally coherent, capable of making free choices, controlling important events, etc.

Such confirmation does not take place at all in a way widespread on the Internet (for example, repeating myself to the mirror "I am a winner"), but it is milder and can take many forms.

One example will be expressing (telling) the values we identify with and which are important to us (for example, pro-ecological activities).

## Compensate

Compensation in the context of self-esteem is called quick, immediate actions aimed at increasing the momentary self-esteem. Most often we can observe:

- rejection of information that threatens our self-assessment (for example, saying that the person who assesses us is incompetent or that the test was biased)
- redirecting attention to other areas (for example, "saving down" comparisons).

The opposite reaction to compensation is a breakdown in self-esteem - that is, simply lowering it due to some threatening information.

## We repair ourselves

The last of the possibilities that we automatically make to maintain our self-esteem in good condition is simply self-repair. So, in a situation where we start to feel that our results are, for example, worse than the results of our loved ones - we go to hard work to increase the level of results achieved.

We often illusionary think that this should be our

reaction. Especially often, parents compare their children with others to "motivate" them to self-repair reactions and improve their results.

However, this is one of the most difficult options available, hence a lot more likely when comparing a child with classmates will be, for example, lowering self-esteem, disgusting people to whom it has been compared or losing interest in the field in which it was compared at all.

## Self-assessment raising and protection – techniques

Strong and positive self-esteem is a sign of a healthy approach to yourself - after all, every person is valuable and has some advantages.

Often, when looking for ways to increase self-esteem, we can come across advice such as "don't compare yourself with others", "appreciate your successes", "believe in yourself" - unfortunately, in this case, causes and effects are confused.

People with high self-esteem believe in themselves

and appreciate their successes, but it will not be so easy for an uncertain person to "believe in himself".

Fortunately, there are techniques by which we will learn to notice the positive sides of our actions. Such training will introduce this type of thinking into a habit, which will result in high self-esteem.

It is important to be systematic and choose techniques that you will feel good with and that will just suit you.

If you struggle with low self-esteem for a long time, do not be afraid to meet with a specialist - an experienced therapist will help you learn techniques that will be right for you.

## Technique 1: A list of strengths

One of the simplest and most commonly used methods, perfect to start with.

It is simply about creating a list of your strengths (in every field). This allows you to get used to positive talking and thinking about yourself. It is worth keeping this list and returning to it.

## Technique 2: A whole jar of success

For this technique, you will need a jar or other container as well as sticky notes and a pen.

Every time you succeed, write it on a piece of paper, fold it and put it in the jar. Just observing the increasing number of notes in the jar is helpful.

In addition, in moments of self-doubt and thinking "I am not successful" you can draw cards and read them to prove yourself that it is different.

## Technique 3: Gratitude journal

This technique allows you to practice the habit of noticing positives.

It is about systematically recording positive events and feelings, just everything that evokes a state of "gratitude".

Thanks to such notes (ideally if they are everyday) you will learn to "capture" successes in everyday life to remember them and then save them.

In addition, a few minutes of thinking in the gratitude category will help your well-being. Such a diary will be (just like the jar before) a lifeline in times of doubt and bad mood.

## Technique 4: Take a compliment from yourself

You don't need any materials to perform this exercise. Just stand in front of the mirror and tell yourself a compliment.

Warning! It may be small and seemingly insignificant, but it is important that it be honest. It can relate to your characteristics (e.g. "I have nice hair", "I am funny") or be praise for achievements (e.g. "today I did a good deed", "I went to the gym even though I didn't want to").

## Technique 5: Celebrate your successes

This technique is about learning how to celebrate your achievements, which contributes to paying more attention to them - and, consequently, strengthening self-esteem.

Reward yourself within your capabilities - small pleasures are enough.

## Technique 6: Correct what is bothering you

It is important to set a realistic level for improving your real shortcomings.

This method is difficult, but the satisfaction resulting from these achievements will have a strong and lasting reflection in self-assessment (remember to reward yourself for achievements!).

## Technique 7: Don't generalize - the devil is in the details

This method is ad hoc - it is useful in times of the so-called "hole" when you feel extremely insecure.

Try to analyze the situation that threatens your self-assessment in as much detail as possible.

When you start with the words "I'm hopeless" they are actually very depressing, but they don't really carry any information.

Redrafting these words and adding details (for example, "I failed, I had to finish the project to work today, but I misjudged my options and will have to ask to postpone the deadline by a week ") will reduce emotional character and increase the possibility of finding a solution or learning for the future.

## Technique 8: Organize your surroundings

The way we look at ourselves has a big impact on how our loved ones look at us.

Note whether there are people around you who discredit your achievements and "pull you down"? If so, try to talk to that person or even limit contact with them.

Also remember that if someone somehow assesses you, it does not have to be true. If someone calls you a chair, that doesn't mean you're one, right? Likewise, you don't have to believe if someone calls you lazy, stupid or unattractive.

Self-esteem is greatly influenced by experience - even those early in childhood . If you notice signs of low self-esteem in your child, it is worth reacting now and teaches your child to like yourself (this skill will be useful throughout your life).

## How to support building self-esteem in a child?

- Do not compare a child with others, because he will learn to do the same (and this is a simple way to reduce self-esteem)
- Give the child as many opportunities as possible to show independence and make their own choices - even the possibility of choosing the clothes or fairy tales to watch by themselves will allow the child to develop a sense of internal control over his life
- Appreciate your child - notice his successes, praise for his effort and creativity
- Celebrate successes with your child - but don't set prices in advance (promising, e.g. a gift for

a good grade, can make your child learn prizes, not because of internal motivation). Every once in awhile (or with greater achievement) take the child for ice cream and tell him clearly that he deserved his success

- Give your child time and attention, try to show that his problems are also important (avoid selling and diminishing his problems, e.g. saying that real problems will only start in adulthood)

## *Techniques - games to strengthen self-esteem in a child:*

### I'm PROUD

To carry out this technique you need a board (for example cork board) - it is best if it hangs permanently in the child's room. Let him systematically attach his successes to the board (e.g. in the form of drawings or something that is associated with a given success).

## ADVERTISEMENT

In this game, the child is supposed to advertise himself, for example, as a good friend , a great daughter or a beloved grandson.

## HANDS

In this game, the child and another participant or participants (they can be his friends, siblings, parents, etc.) get two hands cut out of paper.

Everyone has the task of writing their five strengths on one of their hands (on each finger), and then take the other person's hand and write the person's five strengths. These hands are worth keeping (you can pin them on the board from the first point).

In addition to strengthening the awareness of your child's good qualities, such games are also an ideal opportunity to look at how the child thinks about himself and at what level his self-esteem is currently.

# CHAPTER FIVE

## Keys to generating and maintaining a positive mental attitude

A positive mental attitude allows us to make a difference, what Cervantes did with his novel, which has left a mark in history and is one of the great works of humanity, leaving forever a small gap in hope in the midst of so much realism and pessimism.

## The keys to having a positive mental attitude

This last situation, the small slot of hope, can be a point of light that allows us to stop self-sabotage and complain because of lost opportunities: this light can help us to find solutions and to get the best profit possible.

Being positive does not mean having to be happy and funny at any time of the day. We cannot be happy every moment, but we must not be continually unhappy. It is therefore important not to give up, to keep hope, to see the glass half full and not to focus on the black dot in the middle of a blank sheet.

However, to adopt this attitude, it is important to know how to do it. That's why we offer you these few keys. If we have the right mentality and some ability to manage our thoughts and attention, it will not be difficult for us to adopt a positive attitude that allows us to see the world with a less pessimistic look.

## Do not confuse pessimism and realism

The psychologist Arturo Torres offers us a series of keys to installing a positive mental attitude in our way of life. The first, in connection with what we said in the previous paragraph, is related to realism, which should in no way add a tone of pessimism.

*"Defeat yourself from sadness and melancholy. Life is kind, it has a few days and we must enjoy it now. "*

*-Federico García Lorca-*

When everything seems to be crumbling around us,

the reality seems to be even more sinister and negative. However, if we allow ill-being to flood each of our thoughts, everything around us will eventually acquire this color in our eyes, even if it is not really the case. Thus, to deform and disfigure is a trap that we tend to ourselves.

## Look for concrete goals

Realism is not synonymous with pessimism, illusions and impossible dreams. We have in our hands the power to mark a path full of concrete goals that can be achievable. Thus, to reach one would be a motive of joy and happiness and the latter would be the fuel that would help us to move towards the next, with more strength and envy. In other words, by acting mentally in this way, we will get a very powerful source of motivation.

## Surround yourself with positive people

Of course, the entourage is a base. If the people at our side share a positive attitude, we will more easily achieve a spirit of joy and optimism. This is how the entourage manages to stimulate and motivate us. In the opposite case, of course, the result will be diametrically opposed.

## Look for long-term projects

Setting achievable goals is a good thing, but achieving them must take us somewhere. Towards long-term projects. A series of simple, united goals give life to a much greater purpose, the finality of our life.

Think about what you want to build and turn it into reality. Give a logic or a backdrop to the here and now. Make sure that what you are going to do helps you move towards larger, often transcendent goals, such as personal development. A well-marked now is already a great pillar for future happiness and well-being.

# CHAPTER SIX

## What happens to your brain when you participate in a positive conversation?

Few activities can fill us with a level of sound energy as high as positive conversations can do. These are dialogues in which you feel listened to and want to listen to each other. The words make "click" and lie. They say a lot and their echo turns into a shadow: kind and joyful. This type of conversation is an authentic balm for life.

The opposite is also happening. When you speak, you feel that we do not understand you; you feel upset at having to listen to each other. There are negative messages between the lines. There are also sometimes direct aggression. These meetings leave you only irritated and with a certain bitterness.

We all know from experience that a positive conversation is a wonderful gift. What is new is that science has confirmed this through different studies. What has been demonstrated is that a constructive dialogue has the capacity to modify certain brain patterns. The contribution of this type of conversation is also reflected in neurochemistry.

*"One is looking for someone who can help him give birth to his thoughts, another is looking for someone to help: that's how a good conversation comes up."*

*-Friedrich Wilhelm Nietzsche-*

## A search on words

Mark Waldman and Andrew Newberg are two researchers on human behavior. The former is a professor of communication and a member of the MBA Executive Program at the University of California. The second is the director of the Myrna Brind Center for Integrative Medicine at Thomas Jefferson University. Both did extensive research and wrote a book called "Words Can Change Your Brain ".

The researches of these two experts contain very interesting data concerning words and positive conversations. They discovered for example that the word "no" activates the production of cortisol. The latter is the stress hormone. This puts us in a state of alert and it weakens our cognitive abilities.

On the contrary, the word "yes" causes the release of dopamine. This is a cerebral hormone that regulates the mechanisms of gratification. It helps to produce a feeling of well-being. It also strengthens the positive attitude in communication.

## Words and positive conversation

The theme of the words "yes" and "no" is only a small part of the research done by Waldman and Newberg. Through different experiments, they managed to scientifically prove that words change our brain. Of course, positive or negative conversation as well.

In fact, they realized that some people use words that have negative effects on the brain. Others, on the other hand, use more constructive words. In both cases, it is made aware of the consequences that imply. What is certain is that people leave different sensations in their interlocutors.

## Positive conversation and compassionate

## communication

Waldman and Newberg have developed a concept that is already raging. They call it "Compassionate Communication". This refers to this type of communication in which the most important thing is respect for others and sincerity. It's just the type of communication that takes place when you get involved in a positive conversation.

The researchers also discovered one of the cognitive ingredients that characterize a positive conversation. People understand better when ideas are separate and not more than four at a time. In other words, there is a better guarantee of understanding when one does not deal with several subjects at the same time. Sequences should not include more than four subjects. Besides, a time frame of 30 to 40 seconds is required to move from one theme to another.

Waldman and Newberg also discovered that some words have a profound impact on people. Classically the words poverty, illness, loneliness or death. Such expressions affect the amygdala and facilitate the development of negative thoughts. On the other hand, they also discovered that the effect they produce could be nuanced. It is sufficient that these words are not at the beginning or end of a sentence. Since it is impossible to eliminate the negative words of life, it is appropriate to compensate for them with positive words. The same goes for conversations. When an interaction has been negative, it must be compensated with a positive conversation. This balances not only the interaction but also brain chemistry.

# CHAPTER SEVEN

## Cognitive-Behavioral Techniques to Fight against Intrusive Thoughts

Cognitive-behavioral techniques are very useful for removing power from intrusive thoughts. Those that invade our mind until we fill with their toxic fog, negative and almost always disabling. Thus, before intensifying our anxiety even further and drifting towards an unhelpful cognitive decline, applying these simple strategies on a daily basis will always be of great help.

Those who have never heard of cognitive-behavioral therapy will be interested to know that this is one of the most used "toolboxes" in any psychologist's usual practice. One of the pioneers in this type of strategy has undoubtedly been Aaron Beck who, after having used psychoanalysis for several years, realized the need for another point of view.

The majority of people who were suffering from depression, anxiety, stress or dealing with any type of trauma had a second obsessive, negative and insistent "me" in them that plunged them into the continuous negative dialogue that does not lead to great progress. Such was the interest of Dr Beck. He sought to understand and solve this type of dynamics and changed his therapeutic line to a much more useful one.

Cognitive-behavioral techniques have been incredibly effective in clinical practice. In this way, if we gradually change our patterns of thinking, we will reduce the negative emotional charge that often paralyzes us so that we can ultimately create change and make our behaviors healthier.

## Cognitive Behavioral Techniques for Intrusive Thoughts

Having obsessive and negative thoughts is one of our greatest sources of suffering. It is a way to further intensify the cycle of anxiety, to maintain the well that traps us while we surround ourselves with images, impulses and reasoning that are not very useful that deprive us completely of our feeling of control.

In this case, it is useless to hear "calm down and do not think about things that have not happened yet". Whether we like it or not, the mind is an incessant fabric of ideas and, unfortunately, what it produces is not always good and does not always help us to achieve goals or feel better.

In spite of everything, and we must also say it, we all have, at the end of the day, quite absurd and useless ideas: however, under normal conditions, we do not give much importance to these reasoning's because we prefer to prioritize those who motivate us and those who are useful to us.

When we are going through periods of stress or anxiety, it is common for intrusive thoughts to appear more frequently and to give them the power they do not deserve. Now let's see what cognitive-behavioral techniques can help us in these cases.

## Thought registers

The thought registers allow us to apply logic to a large number of mental processes. For example, consider an employee who is afraid of losing his job.

Overnight, he begins to obsessively think that his bosses or the management team are convinced that everything he does is wrong, wrong or lacking in quality.

Entering this cycle of thought may end up provoking a self-fulfilling prophecy. In other words, by thinking that everything he does is done badly, sooner or later he will end up doing it (for example, falling into a very negative state of mind). Thus, to have a greater sense of control, balance and consistency, there is nothing better than to record the thoughts that paralyze us.

For that, it is enough to note every negative idea which appears in our mind and to try to think of its veracity or not.

*"I'm sure everything I did at work was useless" -> Is there anything to show that this is true? Has anything been reported to me? What I did today is different from what I did the other days for me to think that it is of poor quality?*

## Programming positive activities

Another of the cognitive-behavioral techniques helpful in these cases is programming rewarding activities throughout the day. Something as simple as providing quality time can lead to very positive results and will allow us to break the cycle of ruminating negative thoughts.

These activities can be very simple and short-lived: go out drinking a coffee with a friend, allow us to rest, buy a book, prepare a good meal, listen to music, etc.

## The hierarchy of my concerns

Intrusive thoughts are like smoke from a chimney, the heat of something burning in us. This internal pyre represents our problems, those that we do not find solutions and that, day after day, we create more malaise.

- A first step in controlling this source of

thoughts, feelings and anxieties is to clarify things. And how do we clarify them? By making a hierarchy of problems, a scale of concerns that will go from the smallest to the largest.

- We will begin by writing all that concerns us on a sheet, that is to say, that we will "visualize" all the chaos that there is in us like a storm of ideas.

- Then we will make a hierarchy beginning with the problems that we will consider as minor until we reach the most crippling. The one who, in appearance, dominates us.

Once we have a visual order, we will try to think about each point, to rationalize and find a solution at each level.

## Emotional reasoning

Emotional reasoning is a very common type of distortion. For example, if I had a bad day and feel frustrated, it is that life, simply, is nothing but an endless tunnel. Another common idea is to think that if someone disappoints me, deceives me or abandons me, it's because I do not deserve to be loved.

This is one of the other very useful cognitive-behavioral techniques that we must learn to develop on a daily basis. We cannot forget that our punctual emotions do not always indicate an objective truth: it is only momentary states of mind that we must succeed in understanding and managing.

*"If our thoughts remain bogged down because of biased symbolic meanings, illogical reasoning and misinterpretation, in truth, we become blind and deaf. "*

*-Aaron Beck-*

## Prevention of intrusive thoughts

Whether we like it or not, there are always situations that make us fall back into the abyss of our intrusive thoughts. One way to be alert to these circumstances is to keep a diary to make records. Something as simple as writing our feelings on a daily basis, noting what goes through our head or when these states and internal dynamics arise will allow us to become aware of certain things. There may be people, habits or scenarios that cause us to lose control, feelings of vulnerability, concern or anger.

## CHAPTER EIGHT

### How to have a positive attitude at work?

It is sometimes difficult to have a positive attitude to work, even if it pleases us a lot. Nothing reaches the measure of our needs. We encounter situations where the work environment becomes heavy, where a new leader prints a level of demands leading to stress. On the other hand, there are obviously times when the activity becomes routine and where we count the remaining minutes to end our day.

Positive attitude to work refers to an optimistic and enthusiastic attitude directed not only towards our work activity but also towards all the people involved in it. Cultivating this attitude helps us a lot as it makes a decisive contribution to making our work enjoyable. Likewise, it means that periods of crisis are not experienced in a severe way.

We spend a lot of our life working. Sometimes we spend more time on this than on our loved ones or other activities that we are passionate about. Therefore, our wellness staff depends largely on work experience. So it is worth trying to build and maintain a positive attitude at work. How to achieve it? Let's see some tips that can help us.

## Increase quality to foster a positive attitude at work

One of the things that motivate us the most and helps us develop a positive attitude knows we are doing our job well. And all the more so when we see the results and realize that we are evolving. To improve things, it is important to consider the following aspects:

- Understand what the requirements and skills the work requires and strive to adapt
- Look for methods to perform our tasks more efficiently
- Propose ambitious goals. Not only realize, but also identify what is the next step in the evolution of work
- Know the company, identify its policies, philosophy and structure

If we believe that work is a way to be better, it will

be easier to adopt a positive attitude. A large part of negative attitudes come when we perceive that what we are doing is not worth it or that we are stuck.

## Develop positive and proactive behaviors

Even in the most isolated jobs, there is always a time when we need to connect or coordinate work with others. Therefore, it is not only necessary to cultivate a positive attitude towards the tasks we perform, but also towards the people, we work with as a team. The following behaviors and values will help us to achieve this:

- To be responsible and punctual. People who show apathy or lack of seriousness in their activities and schedules generate some discomfort at work by their behavior
- Courtesy above all. Kind words and gestures are the basis of a good relationship
- Honesty. Trying to prove something that we are not, telling lies or not admitting our mistakes is something that, in the long run, is very detrimental to the working relationship

- Learn to handle the conflict. There will always be differences of opinion, but this should not become a conflict. In particular, it is necessary to learn to state disagreements, without harming or hurting anyone.

When the work environment is positive, motivation increases automatically. If we manage to cultivate good relationships, we will not feel like working with anonymous colleagues, but sharing with collaborators with whom we have a common cause.

## CHAPTER NINE

### Motivation

The word 'motivation' comes from Latin (Latin moveo , movere ) and means 'to set in motion', 'to push', 'to move' and 'to carry'. The term "motivation" is like a cluster of two words: theme +

action, so to take action, you need a goal. The American psychologist Robert Woodworth is considered the formal creator of the concept of motivation, while in the sphere of empirical research - Edward Tolman - the author of purposeful behaviorism. When talking about motivation, one usually thinks about the causes of all actions, needs, drives and motivations of behavior.

## Motivation - characteristics

There is no clear definition of motivation. There is a whole bunch of different theoretical approaches and definitions in psychology. Generally speaking, the definition of motivation in psychology says that motivation is the definition of all processes involved in initiating, directing and maintaining physical and mental human activity. The forms of motivation are different, but they all include mental processes that stimulate, allow choice and direct behavior.

Motivation explains perseverance, despite adversity. In psychology, the concept of "drive" is usually used to describe motivation resulting rather from biological needs, emphasizing its importance for survival and procreation.

The motivational process consists in generating an internal state of readiness to act, stimulating energy, directing the effort to the goal, selectivity of attention (ignoring irrelevant stimuli and focusing on the most important aspects of the situation), organizing reactions in the integrated pattern and continuing activities until conditions change.

## Motivation - types

Typology of motivation can be distinguished in psychology. The basic division takes into account motives (conscious goals) and drives (biological needs). Below are other classifications of incentive processes:

- **Internal motivation** - an individual engages in action for the very action in the absence of an external reward. This type of motivation has its source in the internal characteristics of man, e.g. personality traits, special interests and desires. The concept of internal motivation is often understood as self-motivation, i.e. motivating oneself.

- **External motivation** - a person undertakes to perform a task in order to achieve rewards or avoid punishment, i.e. for "external benefits", e.g. in the form of money, praise, promotion at work, better grades at school. Self-discipline is not dictated by the elimination of internal tension.

- **Conscious motivation** - man is aware of it and can control it.

- **Unconscious motivation** - does not appear in consciousness. Man does not know what underlies his behavior. The importance of unconscious motivation is emphasized by the psychoanalytical theory of Sigmund Freud.

- **Positive (positive) motivation** - is based on positive reinforcements (rewards) and is associated with "pursuit of".

- **Negative (negative) motivation** - is based on negative reinforcements (punishments) and is associated with avoidance, and thus the behavior of "pursuit of".

## Motivation - at work

Motivation at work is an essential aspect of the development of our working life. Although initially, this is an element that should be present, the reality is that in many cases, it is not.

Fortunately, the good news in these cases is that we talk about a psychological situation that can be improved if we make some changes.

Let's think that our emotions are closely linked to the development of workplace functions; emotions which, in turn, are also closely linked to motivation. Moreover, and unfortunately, there is a high percentage of workers who are not satisfied with the work they do, and this is undoubtedly one of the factors that most penalize their motivation at work.

## Motivation techniques at work

Using permanent job motivation techniques will allow us to find out what kind of positions we like best, how we can tailor our current work to our tastes, and how to make those who work with us feel motivated by their tasks.

### 1. Properly insert worker into position

The correct insertion of the worker in his workplace implies the ideal location according to his knowledge and skills. The most appreciated values are confidence and autonomy at work. This autonomy provides greater involvement, commitment, self-assessment, and stimulates skills to find solutions to everyday problems.

Besides, by applying this principle, we are giving the worker a place and creating an emotional environment that favors his development.

### 2. Establish a good work risk plan

Work risk planning and health promotion should be part of the company, not as external actions, but as part of an approach based on comfort and reducing stress levels, without neglecting hygiene and other factors most directly involved in risk protection.

With this principle, we take care of the health and safety of the worker, creating a safe and comfortable physical environment for the development of their functions.

## 3. Apply acknowledgments and incentives

One of the factors that psychology attributes to good self-esteem, a greater ability to offer the best of ourselves and to love what we do is recognition: as social beings, we need others to validate us, recognize us, and recognize the product of our effort. Thus, it is important to recognize work well done, both individually and in groups.

On the other hand, well-used incentives - when misused can have the opposite effect - can accelerate worker performance in certain job responsibilities. These incentives may not be directly related to the financial aspect: there are many ideas and solutions in this regard, such as bonuses, event passes, the possibility of receiving highly specialized and differentiated training, etc.

## 4. Social benefits of the post

Social benefits consist of part of the worker's salary being translated into free services and benefits that allow them to face daily difficulties: health and dental insurance, life insurance, pension plan, daycare, meal ticket, school aid, etc.

Many companies, in the crisis years when wages remained frozen, implemented a social benefit system to compensate for the loss of the status quo. This type of aid is highly valued by workers, especially in times of economic hardship when access to resources is more limited.

## 5. Approach employees and colleagues

A good leader must have the necessary proximity to guide workers, and this role involves concern for the personal well-being of their employees. This interest must be sincere, the result of relationships cultivated from trust and closeness.

## 6. Improve professional performance

Unfortunately, many workers develop their occupation without clear objectives, without the necessary tools or with little planning and support from the organization.

Therefore, worrying about what it takes to get results, or simply wondering from time to time what we can do to improve the workspace or business effectiveness, are simple actions that improve other people's performance.

## Motivation - self-motivation

Where does self-motivation come from, that force so real and powerful that it makes us make extraordinary efforts to achieve our purposes? Where does this feeling of ability come from? Our inner voice is responsible.

That voice, self-motivation, has the power to

enforce the essential everyday actions such as work, study, walk ... Our minds and our thoughts have enough strength to give us enthusiasm and feed the passion we need to start our goals.

It is estimated that on average the mind processes 60,000 thoughts a day. That is about 40 thoughts per minute. We think and react mentally to circumstances or times we live depending on countless emotional variables. Many of these thoughts go unnoticed, and we try to keep some that try to escape and others that unknowingly become part of our reality.

We started from very young to form opinions about ourselves and the space around us. Opinions become ideas, judgments, or concepts that a person has or builds about something or someone.

Opinions are respectable; they come from the diversity of each individual. This does not mean that each opinion is true! Objectively, it is impossible to guess those 60,000 thoughts we talked about earlier. They are only personal judgments, without guarantee of validity. Many of these thoughts and opinions help us reflect, inspire, and shape self-motivation. Others sabotage us by taking away our well-being, becoming factors that demotivate us.

## Self-Motivation and Motivating Factors

However, just as there are "demotivating factors," there are others that motivate us, drive us, and make us feel capable. How to create this impulse so that it can positively influence our mood? How to make our "motivating factors" have greater weight? How do we feel able without the need for outside voices?

*Motivating Factors: 7 Ways to Motivate Yourself*

Let's encourage them to create this much-needed self-motivation to meet any challenge you set yourself in life:

## Inner dialogue

To not accept any thought as absolute truth, create a healthy internal dialogue. We need to know how to differentiate which thoughts will help us reach our goals. Yes, at first it is difficult. You can create an imaginary character, give a name and have dialogues with him. Sometimes you will have to set boundaries, sometimes calm it down ... but over time you can create a lifelong friendship.

## Become aware of your mood

We live within our spirits, some more productive and constructive than others. Self-pity will help you cope with painful times, knowing that when you decide you will have tools to change them. Practice exercises that connect your mind and body, such as yoga or mindfulness.

## Moving from obligations to decisions

How many thoughts start with "I have to"... It's time to make a decision and turn it into an "I will". Make a list of these "I have to..." and you will find that many come from a routine you have created yourself, from legacy customs or from rules that are not necessary for your daily life. How many of these

"I have to..." is a personal decision?

## Work your values

Personal values are deep convictions that determine your way of being and guide your conduct. When they move into action and behavior, they are compelling. For each "demotivating factor" there is a personal value that balances us, strengthens us.

## Create a positive learning attitude

You are part of this world. If what we want to achieve is self-motivation, the obsessive pursuit of perfection doesn't help in the long run. Thus, a positive attitude towards learning contemplates error as part of its process. You learn and adapt. The moment you accept your imperfections, the first step towards excellence is taken.

## Work excellence

When we exercise this skill as a habit, we feel the satisfaction of achieving what we want without comparing ourselves with others. You don't have to compete with anyone, because excellence makes you better every day. With demand, but also with understanding.

## Trust and have faith in you

Trust you, start little by little. It is not because in the past you have tried and failed that now you will not succeed. Have faith, because every moment we act the best we can. Believe in yourself!

Remember one important thing: Self-motivation comes from within; it is built on the strengths and virtues each possesses. Do not give up at the first attempt, or the second, nor does the third ... Every step you take to prove that it can improve. Do not underestimate yourself. Mistakes will be present in your life; it's just up to you to turn them into valuable learning. As long as you feel like turning them into strengths, failure will never exist.

Self-motivation is born in the present. It is at this very moment that faith in your possibilities will be the seed for this Abraham Lincoln phrase to be part of your path.

## How to increase motivation?

Motivation is an indispensable condition for achieving our goals. Motivation is the driving force that emerges from within and helps us to resolve the obstacles we may encounter, to overcome ourselves in our task and successfully achieve what we set out to do.

Motivation drives us in one direction or another, depending on our needs and goals. However, the first step toward success is the willpower we direct to achieve our goals.

Once we have clear what we want, motivation helps us to keep a certain balance and to set in motion the actions needed for the future.

There are different types of motivation: professional motivation, personal motivation, motivating others, motivating students, etc. But the motivation we are going to deal with here is a result of what one really has to do to motivate or motivate someone in any situation whatsoever.

## *Advice to increase motivation*

## Positivism

Being positive is the best option to motivate others or yourself. It is the best option to move on and take strength from where we do not have. Not everything will be a bed of roses, and it is better that way. This will force us to see the positive side of things, to overcome ourselves and to follow the right path.

Instead of complaining and focusing on what we do not like in a situation, let us focus our attention on the positive and what we can learn from the experience we are going through.

## Commitment

What you want to achieve requires a commitment. We are talking about something serious. If you want to achieve something, really commit yourself, set a date!

If we are motivating someone, make them aware of this kind of commitment. Usually, we tend to commit ourselves to words, but not to actions. We become vague and relaxed, which consequently manifests itself in the frustration of not getting what we wanted. Let's be serious about what we want.

## Competition

Competition, in the strict sense of the word, can be understood to mean overcoming others at all costs. This is not what we are talking about.

This kind of competition is a friendly competition, not to step on others, but to be the best version of ourselves. It is our goal, not the goal of others. Being first does not mean being the best. Keep that in mind.

Use competition to support you, to motivate yourself, to use it as a good thing. Competitive people often become selfish, do not help others and just want to overcome them. Here you want to surpass yourself, not others. It only matters to you and your goal. Keep this very clear.

## The importance of a diary

This does not mean writing down what you did during the day, but keeping a record of your progress and setbacks. A journal will help you get organized, know the next step, solve problems that have arisen, and analyze them to put your solution into practice.

Writing your goal and reading it every day several times can also be a foothold.

## View goal

One key to motivation is to visualize yourself reaching your goal. How do you see yourself then? How will you feel? Thinking about it will help keep you motivated and not discouraged by the problems that may arise.

## Daily inspiration

Inspiration is very important so that the path towards your goal will bear fruit. It is not necessary to wait for it to appear out of nowhere; we can get it! At where? Anywhere. Feel receptive to find inspiration in anything, place, event... Enjoy it.

## Reward yourself

Not everything is work, work and work. When you reach a goal, when you can overcome an obstacle that brings you closer to your goal, breathes and give yourself a reward. It can be a little rest, something you wanted to buy, a little trip, whatever. You need to reward yourself for those little things you get. For what? So that motivation does not diminish so that you remain active and strong in your purposes.

These are some of the steps we should take to stay motivated or motivate someone. It is clear that the list is large and can extend as long as we like. It is also true that depending on your personality, some things may work and some may not.

## Love as a source of motivation and enthusiasm

We know that love heals everything, that love heals wounds and creates new visions of the future, but... what happens when we love or feel loved? When we love someone and the other feels loved, a feeling of acceptance and trust is formed that provides the ideal motivation to do our best and be better people. Love as a source of motivation and enthusiasm makes us better.

Being loved makes us feel the safe, belief in ourselves and trust in our potential. Unconditional love generates in us a motor, which opens doors and possibilities for expression. Feeling loved is a reinforcement that enhances our well-being as it means that someone enjoys our company the way we are. This is why love invites us to show ourselves in a sincere and authentic way.

*"Love is the recognition of the potential of the beloved and acts as transforming energy. The look*

*and love of another give us life and helps us transform ourselves. "*

*-Elsa Punset-*

Love gives us life and makes us shine, love makes us trust and develop our potential. It makes us better and helps our skills grow without prejudice and without fear of showing them. It doesn't have to be love between couples that revitalizes us,; for example, the love that parents show their children also makes them grow with confidence and security.

## The brain of the one who has and expresses love

When we love, we generate in each other a wonderful sense of peace and security. We expect the best from others and trust that they will respond to us in the same way, without projecting fears or distrust, only our best wishes and the positive we see in those we appreciate. When we offer love, we promote good self-esteem thanks to the bubble of calm and tranquillity we created in this exchange.

What really happens in the brain when we love?

Thanks to neuroimaging techniques, Andreas Bartels and Semir Zeki of University College London conducted a study in which they observed the brain activity of some people when they saw pictures of their loved ones and when they saw pictures of their friends so that they could study the differences. And compare them.

They found, thanks to this technique and this study, that when we fall in love or love our children, we disconnect parts of the brain related to other emotions and, above all, our capacity for social criticism.

They also noted that when we look at our beloved, there are parts of the prefrontal cortex and certain areas related to aggression, fear, or planning that disconnect. This affects our judgment as we tend to rely more upon and be less strict on our social assessment. We could say that our brain is programmed, when we love, to see the good of the other.

# Love as a source of motivation to be better

*Scientists say that "the human attachment employs a mechanism that overcomes social distance by deactivating circuits connected to negative emotions and social critical evaluation, and unites individuals through the reward circuit, which explains the power of love as a source of motivation and enthusiasm".*

Therefore, we can say that love makes us better people. Love gives us the strength to meet new challenges as it brings us a person to our side who trusts us, who helps us improves our potential to follow and strive.

Loving, we have the opportunity to create all this in the other; therefore, when we project our love, we generate the best feelings and the best of us in the other. Both were loving and being loved gives us the opportunity to improve and develop security frameworks within us. So what are you waiting to love?

Love as a source of motivation gives us the strength to meet new challenges.

## CHAPTER TEN

### The Psychology of Forgiveness

The psychology of forgiveness is also a form of detachment. It refers to an act of courage whereby people put aside the grudge that consumes them to accept what has happened and move on. It is also a restructuring of the self, a psychological way to redress suffering, negative emotions, and gradually find inner peace.

When we search bibliographies regarding the psychology of forgiveness, we find mainly works and documents related to personal growth, the study of morals, and even the world of religion or spirituality. However, are there scientific studies on what forgiveness is, how to do it, and what it takes for our physical and emotional balance to take this step?

*"The weak cannot forgive. Forgiveness is an attribute of the strong. "*

*- Mahatma Gandhi -*

Yes, there are some studies on the psychology of forgiveness. In fact, the "American Psychological Association" has a lot of work and research on what to forgive or not. Because our ancient and present societies are full of conflict throughout their history, they have not always been able to move forward: a dimension that in turn is the key to our mental well-being.

Certainly, we all have a spiked thorn, a pending account of some fact of our past that restricts our present happiness, which diminishes our ability to build a much more satisfying present. All of us, somehow, keep our small share of resentment toward something or someone who needs healing...

**Forgive to avoid personal "wear and tear"**

The best way to delve into this area of psychology is to differentiate what is forgiveness and what is not. Forgiving in the first place does not mean telling us that what happened at any given time was good if it was not. It also does not mean "accepting" or reconciling with the person who has harmed us; let alone force us to live with or feel sorry for her.

In fact, the psychology of forgiveness offers us the appropriate strategies for us to take the following steps:

**Accept that things happened this particular way**. Nothing that happened at this particular moment in the past can be changed. Therefore, we must stop thinking, lose energy, courage and health, wondering how things could have happened if we had acted otherwise.

*"Forgiving is learning to "let go" to reinvent a new self that takes over the past but has the strength to enjoy the present.*

In turn, the psychology of forgiveness tells us that we are not required to understand or accept the values or thoughts of the person who has harmed us. Forgiveness is not offering clemency or seeking justification for what we suffer. We must never lose our dignity.

**It is necessary to facilitate the grief of resentment**, to "let go" the anger, the intensity of despair and the blockage that prevents us from breathing ... To do so, we must stop hating those who have harmed us.

On the other hand, there is an important aspect that we often forget. Forgiveness is the foundation of any relationship, whether double, friendship, etc. Remember that not everyone sees things the same way; In fact, there are several perceptions, approaches and opinions.

Sometimes we take on certain behaviors such as outrages or acts of contempt when what lies behind is a simple intolerance or misunderstanding. Thus, and to stop seeing betrayals where there are none, we must be able to expand our sense of understanding and our capacity for forgiveness.

## The Psychology of Forgiveness: The Key to Health

Dr Bob Enright of the University of Wisconsin is one of the best-known experts in the study of the psychology of forgiveness. After more than three decades of analyzing cases, doing studies and writing books on the subject, he has concluded something that might catch our attention. Not everyone can do it, not everyone can take the first step toward offering forgiveness. The reason for this lies in the belief that forgiveness is a form of weakness.

This is a mistake. One of the best ideas that forgiveness psychology gives us is that forgiving, taking the first step, and allowing us to move forward more freely in our present, gives us the opportunity to learn new values and strategies to address any source of stress. Forgiving and recycling grudges frees us; It is an act of courage and strength.

Dr. Enright reminds us that there are many reasons to forgive. The best of these is that we will gain health. There are many studies that show the close relationship between forgiveness and reducing anxiety, depression and other disorders that reduce our quality of life.

*The person who remains day after day trapped in the cycle of memories, the clutches of resentment, and persistent hatred of a past event or particular person develops beyond unhappiness chronic stress. No one deserves to live this way. Because there is no more toxic emotion than anger combined with hatred...*

Let us, therefore, put into practice some of the following strategies to ease the path of forgiveness:

- Forgiveness is not forgetting, it is learning to think better and understand that we are not obliged to facilitate reconciliation, but to accept what has happened without feeling "weak" by taking this step. To forgive is to free ourselves from many burdens that we do not deserve to carry throughout our lives.

- Hate takes energy, courage and hope. We must, therefore, learn to forgive in order to survive and live with more dignity.
- Therapeutic writing and keeping a journal can also help us.
- We must understand, in turn, which time alone does not help to forget. Letting go of the days, months and years will not stop us from hating or remembering what happened. We will not leave tomorrow the discomfort we feel today.
- We need to understand that forgiveness is a process. We may never be able to completely forgive the other person, but we can discharge a good deal of all the resentment so we can breathe a little better...

To conclude, the field of forgiveness psychology is very broad and, in turn, has a very close relationship with health and well-being. It is a discipline that offers us fabulous strategies to apply in any area of our life, our work and our daily relationships. Forgiving is, therefore, one of the best skills and virtues we can develop as human beings.

## Myths about Forgiveness

Forgiveness is a powerful weapon that allows you to live in peace with others and especially in peace with yourself. However, many people fail to understand how liberating it can be to forgive others.

Forgiveness can be a double-edged sword. In fact, it's a common way of manipulating others to get you to do what you want. That's why it's important to understand forgiveness well and learn to set boundaries to protect yourself from the abuse of others.

On the other hand, our culture imposes on us certain forms of behavior that we follow mechanically, often without realizing what we are doing or why we do it. We simply react as we are expected to do, without thinking of other options, feeding and reinforcing the stereotypes that displease us so much.

The following are the most widespread

misconceptions and beliefs about forgiveness. Reflecting on these myths will help you to forgive more sincerely and to be more aware of what you do and why.

## You must overcome the feeling of being hurt before forgiving

Many people believe that they must overcome pain and anger first to forgive as if they need to feel better first to be able to forgive. But the reality is just the opposite.

Forgiveness is a choice we must make. If you expect the hassle to pass, it will make the process increasingly difficult. It is with the "hot head" that we must decide. In this way, the state of tension and boredom will pass first because it will not let anger take over.

## 2. You have to choose forgiveness, even if you do not feel it

This is something we try to convey to our children,

and many people still adhere to this premise in adulthood. But forgiveness is not an option that can be imposed on you. It must be a free and conscious choice, even if it takes a little bit longer to meet them.

If you only forgive because you have to do it because you think you have to, but you do not forgive from the depths of your heart, then anger and rage become negativity that eventually seeks an outlet. Take all the time you need, but decide for yourself, whether you forgive or not.

## 3. You should not forgive the same thing again and again

People are people and that means we make mistakes, and sometimes the same. In fact, we are the only creatures that stumble twice over the same stone - so it is said.

Learning from your mistakes is not easy, especially if you are not fully aware of your mistake. After all, not everyone understands everything in the same way and there are many factors that play a role in our behavior.

There are things you can forgive once but find it very difficult to do so a second time. But not all offenses are equally serious and their effect depends on the person who commits them. Therefore you have to look at each problem individually and should not generalize.

## 4. You can not forgive anyone who has not regretted

If the person does not regret what he has done, then all the weight of anger and anger will break over you. It will actually hurt a lot more. However, if you manage to forgive a person who has hurt you, you will free yourself from this heavy burden.

Many people use this to hurt others because they understand the power it has to show no remorse for their actions. But if you forgive them, you will disarm them. You will take them an important means to achieve negative purposes.

## 5. By forgiving, you validate the other person's action

Many people believe that forgiving is a way to tell the other person that what they have done is okay. In fact, many people use this way of thinking to validate inappropriate or illegal actions.

However, you are more likely to tell someone that he no longer has enough power to influence you if you forgive him. You say that you are above these things. In that sense, forgiveness allows you to override the psychological manipulation that the other person is attempting to exercise. This has nothing to do with the validation of an action.

## The Benefits of Forgiveness

Sometimes people around us do things that hurt us and make us feel betrayed or even attacked. In other situations, we are the ones who do something they later regret. It is not always easy to forgive, but it is really healthy. Even if we focus primarily on ourselves, we should learn to forgive. Because forgiveness is not only for our mental health important but also for our physical well-being.

Forgiveness is easier said than done, and we often find it a great challenge. Sometimes we misunderstand them and think that it is about someone being spared, what is happening and being given up to repay the other. But forgiveness is so much more than that. To forgive is to renounce what has happened.

And whatever the situation may be, forgiveness promotes our health.

## Forgiveness is good for the heart

Forgiving promotes the health of our hearts. In a study published in the Journal of Behavioral Medicine, forgiveness has been found to be associated with a lowered pulse and lower blood pressure. The same study showed that forgiving helps reduce stress. So we can specifically contribute to the health of our hearts and to our overall health.

## Forgiveness is good for our physical and mental health

A later study found a link between forgiveness and five parameters of health: physical symptoms, medications taken, depth of sleep, tiredness, and physical discomfort. It also seems that we can see a strengthening of our spirituality, our ability to deal with conflict and reduce stress, by reducing the negative effects and symptoms of depression caused by unforgiveness. So, forgiveness has a big impact on our overall health.

## Forgiveness helps to have better relationships with others

Another study, published in the journal Personality and Social Psychology Bulletin, found that forgiveness helps restore positive thoughts, feelings, and behaviors to the person who is being forgiven. This means that when we forgive, we restore the original, positive state of the relationship. In addition, this can lead to positive behavior towards third parties. There is a connection between forgiveness, volunteer work, donations, charity and other altruistic behavior.

## A few final thoughts

When we forgive, we free ourselves from ourselves - from our own bondage. We renounce the pain and bitterness that we have worn on our shoulders like a yoke, enabling us to become free. By forgiving, we conclude with a thing from our past to which we have clung.

Forgiveness also means accepting what has happened. This is how we experience a liberation deep within us - not only from the deeds or accusations of others but also from ourselves. It is not only important to forgive others. It is also important to think about the things we have to forgive ourselves.

To forgive is good for the body, for the mind, for interpersonal relationships and for finding our role in this world. This realization should convince us that it is much better to let go and forgive his wrath.

## The Importance of Forgiveness

Forgiving is essential because it frees us from bad feelings such as rancour, anger and revenge. When negative feelings like these overwhelm a human being, the worst of them is manifest, triggering physical and psychic harm to himself and those around him.

Some individuals remain resentful of others and hold continuous grief for a long time, which is extremely harmful to both. After all, those who do not forgive limit their possibilities of love.

Forgiveness is an opportunity to break free from the negative strings of the past and move on. Thus, forgiving is a liberating action that symbolizes intelligence and allows a person to mature. Not forgiving prevents the chance to live new possibilities and have more satisfaction in personal life.

## Developing the power of forgiveness

Forgiveness does not mean forgetting, but remembering what happened and being at peace with each other and with oneself. By forgiving, it is possible to get rid of the feeling of bitterness that can trap us around a negative memory.

Developing forgiveness requires that even if the memory of the past act comes back to visit thoughts, it does not affect our present or shake our habitual peace. Without it, a person who does not forgive remains stagnant, unable to engage in simple interaction because of a bad feeling.

Although the injustice suffered was great, it should not contaminate us completely. Forgiveness is necessary. It is a great challenge of maturity and experience.

## Reasons to forgive

There are many reasons to forgive. Feelings such as hurt and resentment are tiring both mentally and physically, leading to insomnia, stress, and depression. So forgive, because:

- is good for yourself: you stop focusing excessively on your hurts and can focus more on things that are positive for you;
- takes a weight off your back: you take the stress out of someone else's offense;
- offers a correct view of events: you analyze facts with clear eyes, without hatred and immaturity;
- gives you the chance to live new possibilities: you feel freer to embrace the world and live without fear of trusting others again.

Forgiving is difficult, but it is a very smart action and has many benefits. The feeling generated by forgiveness conveys more tranquility and self-knowledge. In addition, harboring grudges only increases the chance of attracting more enemies and delaying one's life.

It is best to value your time with positive feelings by placing your heart and thoughts on something that makes you happy. Therefore, do not underestimate the power of forgiveness. Forgive the one who hurt you and move on.

## Coaching Tools - The 10 Steps to Forgiveness

Forgiveness is a mental, physical and spiritual process of no longer feeling, or rather resenting, and negative emotions such as anger, fear, grief, and guilt. It is also an act of releasing painful feelings that make us relive suffering each time we remember our mistakes, certain people, and the moments that have caused us deep sorrows, frustrations, and disappointments.

Forgiveness makes us look forward, makes us move forward without the company of old regrets, and has the power to restore our optimism. On the other hand, the more we have to live with grief, the farther we are from illuminating our thoughts, as we often return to our past and plunge into pain and unresolved issues.

Forgiving is especially an act of love for yourself and those who have wronged us. It provides greater physical well-being, increased life satisfaction, emotional balance and makes us fully live our here and now.

**The 10 Steps to Forgiveness**

- **Permission to Forgive** - Forgiveness comes from within, from genuine permission we grant to forgive ourselves and others for any harm they have caused us. This act frees us from negative feelings, stress, and severely cuts off the link with the event/person.

- **Acceptance of Yourself** - Seek to understand who you are in essence and identify why a particular fact causes such pain/anger. With this, try to express your feelings and express your point of view about the situation.

- **Internal Dialogue and Focus on Forgiveness** - Take responsibility for doing your best to achieve self-forgiveness. Seek to dialogue with your feelings and focus on turning your pain into positive emotions and motivation to continue.

- **Understand the Purpose of Forgiveness** - Forgiveness is not accepting one's mistake, but freeing yourself from the harmful feelings that bind you. By forgiving, you restore your peace of mind, your emotional balance, and redeem the positive emotions that were previously immersed in your sorrows.

- **Live the Here and Now** - Understand that it is not what happened, but your interpretation of the fact, yesterday or ten years ago, that causes you to suffer. Do not bring negative emotions from the past to your present. Allow yourself to take new readings and react differently.

- **Allow Yourself To Reassign** - In times of distress, try to exercise self-control as this prevents stress hormones from spreading throughout your body and causing anxiety and distress. Breathe slowly, relax, visualize a new scenario, and imagine another outcome to the situation.

- **Think Positive** - Every behavior, however

bad, has a positive intention. Imagine new ways, new ways to reach your goals, and stop focusing on the error itself. Recall your achievements, your life history, be proud and honor your story.

- **Live with Love** - Decide to live the bright side of life, take the focus off the person who hurt you and avoid brooding over disappointments. Try to see positive attitudes, love, gratitude, and kindness around you.

- **Seek Learning** - Make disappointment opportunities to learn how to deal with your frustrations and forgive yourself and others. No one is foolproof, not even you. Recognize your own failings, learn from them, and always bring something positive into your life.

- **Be True** - Give yourself sincere forgiveness, acknowledge your mistakes, and try not to suffer for it anymore. Likewise, ask forgiveness from those who may have hurt and offended, and allow the other person to be free of the fact as well.

# CHAPTER ELEVEN

## The art of positive thinking to live better

Positive thinking and greater control over the flow of our thoughts is investing in the quality of life. Because the one who controls the voice of negativity is able to directly influence his own emotions. Because those who think and feel positively influence their behavior, their organism, and even their own health. In the end, happiness starts with what happens within ourselves, not outside.

Although we all know these principles, in our daily lives we continue to attach too much importance to this critical voice that loves negativity. It is she who reminds us of yesterday's mistakes. It is this presence that brings us down, leading us to the gates of anxiety, anticipating what may or may not happen if we do this or that. Before we despair over this kind of thinking that often characterizes us, it is worth having a very clear point.

*"No pessimist has ever discovered the secrets of the stars, or opened a new door for the human spirit."*

*Helen Keller*

Neuroscientists remind us that the human brain is programmed to focus on the negative. It is neither a curse nor a punishment imprinted on our DNA. It is our survival mechanism. By anticipating the dangers (even if they are not real), we prepare our bodies to defend ourselves against them. Feelings such as worry, anxiety or anxiety instantly release various chemicals such as cortisol to allow us to always be "alert".

On the other hand, another thing neuropsychologists also tell us is that negative thoughts act like the habit of smoking. Not only impact our health and well-being. They often become impregnated around us, affecting our families, friends, co-workers... Because the brains of those who listen to us also change, they also end up feeling nervous and irritable...

## Think Positive to Train Your Brain towards Wellness

Barbara Fredrickson is a well-known scientist at Stanford University, famous for her studies in positive psychology. As you explain in your studies, overcoming the influence of negativity is a challenge that, once overcome, turns into a profitable investment. More than an art, positive thinking is the result of an ongoing exercise with which to change our brain's "factory" programming.

As we already know, our mind has a natural inclination to focus on the negative side to ensure our survival. Therefore, we must be able to include within us another path, another sophisticated program for investing not only in facing risks but also in investing in well-being, in happiness. In the end, positive thinking generates clarity, balance, and direction. It helps us not to get lost in the swamps of fear to be more proactive, surer of ourselves.

Here's how we can train our brains to learn to think positive.

## 1. Train your attention so she is focused on the present.

Daniel Goleman recalls the importance of training our attention in his book Focus. We should see it almost as a muscle, an entity that we should place at our service, not at the service of a wandering mind. The point is that this basic psychological process is more controlled by ourselves than by external stimuli or anarchic thinking.

- As a curiosity, it is worth remembering that the thought circuit extends along the gyrus of the upper cingulate and the prefrontal medial cortex. Our rationalizations flow through these brain structures. Sometimes this pathway of cells, connections, and neurons is so hyperactive that it is difficult to have control over it. In a short time appear exhaustion, stress, apathy, negativity...
- One way to control thinking is to control our attention. To achieve this, there is nothing better than "disconnecting" this flow of

thoughts. For at least 15 minutes trying not to think about anything. Imagine the surface of a lake, silent and smooth as a mirror. Everything is in balance, there are no sounds. Just calm down.

- Once we can silence the voice of thoughts, we will focus our attention on what is surrounding us. In the present moment.

## 2. Think positive, the art of having a purpose

Positive thinking requires purpose. Negativity and all the noise of unfeasible thoughts are like an aimless cyclone that takes it all away. Therefore, to break with this unproductive mental tendency we must define our purpose.

*I want to feel good, I want to be calm, I want to reach my goals, I want to be well with myself...*

All of these goals follow one direction, one clear sense. So, once we have our attention focused on the present moment, what we will do is enumerate our purposes one by one with conviction. Goal setting is a key to well-being, making sense of life, being fascinated, and letting these positive emotions influence our conduct.

**Train your brain's ability to work with positive information**

Positive thinking does not only require focus, proper attention, purpose, and willingness. It also requires building networks in our brain to remember the importance of working with positive information. What do we mean by that? Basically, even though we say to ourselves, "I have a goal to accomplish," our mind is sometimes still positioned in ancient mechanisms, in a path of negative and unfeasible actions.

- Working with positive information requires eliminating our limiting attitudes.
- In addition, we need to create a more relaxed, more open to experience and more optimistic self. We must put past mistakes aside to see present opportunities.
- Likewise, it will be very important to learn how to use filters to keep only useful

information, the one that helps and stimulates, not the one that puts us once again in our comfort zone.

## CHAPTER TWELVE

### Thoughts destroy but also heal

Health and disease are now seen as a complex balance that arises from the interaction between body and mind, between organism and thoughts. Little by little, we get over the simplistic views that took away the influence of the subjective world on our bodies and therefore on disease and healing.

Conventional medicine is gradually gaining awareness of the limitations of its approach. The twentieth century was marked by a paradigm in which the body-machine idea prevailed. Seen through this view, the organism was like an apparatus made of different parts, and the disease was dysfunction in any of *these parts, both functional and structural.*

*"If you don't act the way you think, you'll end up thinking the way you do."*

*–Blaise Pascal–*

However, thanks to the advances in medicine itself, it can be seen that the inner dimension has a strong influence, whether direct or indirect, on anyone's state of health. In addition, this influence is even more marked on perceived health status. That is why they say those thoughts - with their influence - get sick and kill, but they also heal.

## Pharmacological medicine and the medicine of thoughts

Bruce Lipton is a Ph.D. in Cell Biology and author of several books. He delved into health, illness, and the influence of thoughts on these processes. His findings and reasoning are incredibly interesting.

Lipton points out that pharmacological medicine is virtually a failure. This is because chemical drugs, all of them, cause as many or more adverse effects than the disease itself. He says that even many of these drugs lead to death overtime.

He also stated that the natural environment of the cell is blood and that, in turn, changes in the blood are determined by the nervous system. At the same time, the nervous system is the natural environment of thoughts and feelings. Therefore, from Lipton's point of view, it is thoughts and feelings that ultimately get sick and, consequently, those that also have the possibility of healing help.

## The power of thoughts on the body

It is not just Bruce Lipton, but so many researchers who give enormous power to thoughts in the processes of illness and healing. Even pharmacology-savvy doctors know that if someone has an illness, they are more likely to heal if they stay in a surrounding environment, surrounded by affection and trust.

It is not an esoteric thing, nor an effect from the beyond. The explanation of the power of thoughts is also a matter of chemistry. When a person is in the presence of a pleasant presence or enjoying a positive stimulus, their brain secretes dopamine, oxytocin and a host of health-giving substances to cells. The same happens when the stimulus is negative, causing fear, anger or any other destructive emotion.

The body develops a titanic task every day: producing hundreds of billions of new cells to replace those that die. It also needs to defend itself against thousands of health-threatening pathogens. If your body feels that it has to struggle with highly negative stimuli from the surrounding area every day, it will expend all its energy on it and put aside these other growth and protection functions. The consequence: you get sick more easily.

# CHAPTER THIRTEEN

## How to deal with a moment of sadness

The best way to face a moment of sadness is by accepting that such a moment will exist and trying to understand it. We have the right to be sad from time to time, as well as to live those moments that are a natural part of life. Ideally, just don't let them affect us too intensely.

Dealing with a moment of sadness properly has a lot to do with our attitude toward him. On many occasions, depending on our point of view, our interpretation and willingness to address it, the problem will grow or shrink in magnitude and volume.

Firstly, it is important to talk about this time in which we live in the fantasy that we should always be happy and happy. For some reason, the idea that we have to be happy all the time, smiling, optimistic and in perfect harmony dominated our minds.

We all know that this is impossible. And it is not only impossible, but it would also be inappropriate.

The philosophy of positive thinking cannot become a tyranny of positivity.

This is the first issue we have to keep in mind when we are not having a good time. We are not committing any wrongdoing and there is nothing wrong with us for being at a sensitive or sensitive time.

## Sadness and depression

Anyone who is alive and healthy will have a sad time every now and then. We all eventually go through phases where things get complicated and don't go as we wish.

There are also moments of fatigue, disappointment or boredom. No one lives a perfect enough life to ever go through a difficult time.

There are also losses and frustrated desires that cause us sadness. It is very common for these steps to be confused with depressive periods. Many people say they feel depressed when in fact they are only sad for a specific cause.

Clinical depression is a much more complex and

permanent state than a simple moment or period of sadness or grief. It is necessary to identify the entire symptomatology for a relatively long period. And also that these symptoms cause a noticeable and negative change in one's quality of life.

## To deal with sadness...

It is important to deal with sadness before it grows into the flight, as colloquially said. Rather than overcome it, the goal is to understand it to prevent it from happening.

To reach this goal, the first step is to admit that we are feeling unmotivated and unwell and to give ourselves permission to be. Therefore it is convenient to perform the following actions:

- **Listen to yourself.** Listening to yourself means letting out all the ideas in your head and detecting the emotions they are causing. Admitting that you feel sad and trying to define what makes up your sadness is the way.
- **Speak and write.** Saying what we feel out loud or writing helps to organize ideas.

Outsourcing thoughts is one of the indispensable steps in dealing with a moment of sadness. It may be helpful to simply talk while recording and then listen to your speech.

- **Search for the real reasons.** We often feel sad for very precise reasons, but other times we don't know exactly why. It is always very important to ask yourself what is really behind this feeling.
- **Ask a question to get the answer.** What can I do to get a little better right now? The answer to this question will give you a clue as to what you should do to deal with this moment of sadness.

**Other things to keep in mind when dealing with sadness**

It is very important that you do not judge yourself or be too hard on yourself. There is no reason to stop feeling sad when there is a real reason why you feel that way.

What you can do is put a limit on this mood. Dealing with a sad feeling does not mean ending it right now, but understanding it and preventing it from growing.

Another effective way to cope with a sad period is to put yourself in a "self-care" mode. This means pampering yourself, eating something you like, taking the time to do something that brings you comfort... That is, doing some activity that makes you feel good.

Also, try to think of all the reasons why you feel lucky.

It's always a good idea to take a break from a negative mood. An exercise is a good option for this. All you have to do is walk around some area where you feel comfortable with faster steps and your body will produce some hormones that will help you.

It is also highly recommended that you eat and

hydrate well. This will help make you feel a little better.

Most importantly, you will always be able to express what you are feeling. If you want to cry, simply cry. If not, remember that art is also a fabulous ground for dealing with sadness or any other more troublesome feeling.

# CHAPTER FOURTEEN
## The habit of positive people

Do you know what are the habits of positive people? If you are not a positive person yet, becoming one may seem simple. But often it's not as easy as you think. Choosing a positive way of thinking becomes especially important when we agree with the idea that we are what we think. Thus, if we think positively, if we adopt an optimistic attitude, we will have far more advantages than if, on the contrary, we fall into the temptation of pessimism and defeatism.

Why is it so important to think positively? What are the benefits of being optimistic? Also, what do you have to do to change the chip and start seeing things more positively? Can we really change the way we think and become positive?

*"Anything positive is better than a negative nothing."*

*-Elbert Hubbard-*

**A positive mind is a powerful mind.**

The truth is that a positive attitude can lead us to reach certain heights that would otherwise not be possible to climb. In this sense, acquiring a new way of thinking maybe what will make the difference between who we are and who we want to be.

In many situations, we tend to blame others for our failures and our adversities. We think they contributed to our downfalls. But it's not always so. Next time a project does not evolve or you have a problem, do a personal assessment and scrutiny of the situation. Think that in many cases the mind controls what we do and how we react to people and circumstances.

A positive person can do many things that provide well-being. So what do we get when we choose to think positively rather than fall into the temptation of pessimism? Every individual thought and every decision we make has an impact on our lives.

*"The greatest discovery of all time is that a person can change their future simply by changing their*

*attitude.”*
*-Oprah Winfrey-*

## Change habits to be a positive person

Optimism is a learning trait. So this does not mean that we cannot reprogram our way of thinking, seeing and looking. Fortunately, as research shows, we can teach ourselves to see the world in a more positive way.

To do this, one of the secrets is changing habits. Habits can help us achieve success, or they can be an obstacle and drag us toward failure. Habits, whether good or bad, are inevitable and part of our lives. Ultimately, they can have the power to shape our habitat, shaping much of what we are.

Establishing good habits is not an easy task, even for very successful people. When it comes to finding ways to make good habits become part of our routine, the fight is real. Therefore, being proactive and striving to build good habits is a challenge for anyone.

Trying to be proactive rather than reactive will

increase the chances of creating good habits and becoming a positive person. To begin with, one must keep in mind that it is better to set goals for positive habits rather than trying to eliminate bad habits routines.

**Positive people's habits**

Here are some of the positive people habits you can include in your life to stimulate optimism and become a positive person.

- **Find an optimistic point of view in a negative situation**. One of the simplest but most effective ways to create a positive outlook is to ask yourself more helpful questions whenever possible. The goal is to try to get something good out of the situation: turn the circumstance into opportunity.
- **Cultivate and live in a positive environment.** Choose carefully who you spend your time with and what you do in your day to day life. The people you stay with, what you see, what you listen to, what you read ...

In order to maintain a positive attitude, it is essential to have influences in your life that support and lift you up rather than bringing you down.

- **Take it easy.** When we go too fast, the path usually goes wrong. We think fast, we talk fast, we move fast... Everything goes into a spiral that gives way to a stressful and superficial life. Acquiring positive thinking habits requires slowing down.

- **Stop - Breath - Focus.** Don't make a storm in a glass of water. It is very easy to lose focus, especially if you are stressed and too fast. When you feel negative thinking absorb you, stop, breathe and rearrange your thoughts.

- **Bring positivity around you**. You give what you get. If you add optimism and positivity to the people around you, you will receive the same. The way you treat others and how you think about them also tends to have a big effect on how you treat and think about yourself. Start by helping, listening and smiling.

- **Have a healthy lifestyle.** Do exercises regularly. Eat and sleep well. This will keep your body healthy and your mind free. You will have the energy to control your thoughts and to sense any spark of negativity.

- **Learn to respond to criticism in a healthy way.** The criticism is almost inevitable, both you yourself do as the others do. The key is to learn how to deal with them in a healthy way, starting by making clear what is true and objective about criticism and what is a personal perception or opinion. In any case, one cannot look at criticism as personal and let it go. After all, criticism is not a universal truth. And if you can learn something from them, you can really improve. So enjoy!

- **Start the day in a positive way.** The way you start your morning usually sets the tone for the rest of the day. So be careful about how you spend your mornings.

- **Smile! Positive people smile a lot, always smile.** When you smile, you are bringing optimism, you are showing a good mood, you are showing respect and you are transmitting good vibes. When you smile, you are sending your brain the message that everything is fine. Everything is easier to smile.

## CHAPTER FIFTEEN
### The power of proactive thinking

To take the reins of fate, we must stop reacting to everything that happens to us and dare to act. One way to accomplish this is by applying proactive thinking. It allows us to face reality creatively, responsibly and in tune with life's changes. In essence, it's about finding the motivation to move on.

Often it is said that what defines a leader is precisely your vision and your remarkable ability to turn a vision into reality. Of course, none of us undoubtedly have a 'crystal ball' to anticipate the detail, which may or may not happen within a certain period of time.

However, when facing reality (whether we like it or not), we always have two options: apply reactive thinking or proactive approach. The first defines a type of behavior in which we are limited to reacting exclusively to everything that happens to us. It is like someone who, while walking a path, hits the branch of a tree and screams in pain.

On the other hand, we have another interesting possibility. We should not just limit ourselves to letting certain things happen and dodging the tree branch. We must find another way to cross this danger-filled path. We can, if we so choose, apply proactive thinking to be prepared, have a plan in place, and avoid, as much as possible, being "hit" by circumstances.

Applying this kind of approach has great benefits. Edward de Bono, for example, a reference in the field of creativity, defines proactive thinking as "deliberate reasoning" that we could all train to gain quality of life.

*"Vision is the art of seeing invisible things."*
*- Jonathan Swift –*

## Proactive thinking or aspiring to a more positive (and healthier) future

Psychologists Stephanie Jean Sohl and Anne Moyer of Stony Brook University conducted a very revealing study a few years ago on stress and human well-being. According to this work, people using proactive coping were much less likely to develop high levels of stress.

The correct way to apply proactive thinking, according to this research, is based on two very simple strategies:

- The first is defined as "proactive questions". It would simply clarify some aspects such as: What do I need to feel good in the short and long term? What changes should I make to achieve my personal goals?

- The second strategy is based on the collection of "preventive ideas". It is about devising strategies for how and how to respond to certain things if they happen. For example, if I suspect I might get fired from work, I should think of other exits, having a 'plan b' prepared.

Let's see, however, what other factors define proactive thinking.

### *Proactive Thinking: A Positive, Creative, Flexible Mindset*

Edward de Bono used to explain in his works that sometimes the smartest people are the least proactive. What may at first seem surprising to us has its explanation.

- In order to anticipate effectively, originally and positively for our near future, we must generate many ideas and be creative.
- There are brilliant people who are experts when it comes to an understanding of the very

complex aspects of our reality. However, they are unable to create alternatives or new proposals.

- Proactive thinking needs to go beyond the present moment, requires a visionary and very flexible attitude.
- It is not, therefore, a matter of being 'great thinkers', but 'flexible and very original thinkers'.

**Frustration tolerance**

The frustration is an emotional bomb that explodes inside of us when things do not go as expected. Few psychological tests are so uncomfortable and difficult to deal with. However, it is imperative to learn to tolerate the stones of the path we all encounter along our particular climbs toward a goal.

The proactive person, this profile that applies a deliberate, optimistic, purposeful type of thinking, has learned to live with the feeling of frustration. Of course, on any journey there are difficulties, and for this reason, it is necessary to foresee and find ways to overcome these obstacles along the way.

So one thing we must understand in proactive thinking is that, as far as possible, we need to learn to deal with this surprise nuance that the future can bring us through innovative plans.

## Reality is full of patterns

Life has its standards. We may not appreciate them at first, but they are there, latent, orchestrated by this daily flow where there are things that can be anticipated, where there are stimuli that trigger processes and actions that bring consequences.

The proactive person, therefore, is someone who has learned to observe, analyze, and arouse his intuitive view of things. Little by little, she realizes that there are certain nuances that don't happen just because. Understanding patterns is a way of being prepared, thinking of response strategies to live better.

To conclude, if we have been limiting ourselves to simply reacting to facts rather than being proactive for some time, we need to rest. When we go through a large number of events, it is ideal to pause momentarily to process what has happened, to regain our spirits, energy, and strength.

## CHAPTER SIXTEEN
### How to identify automatic negative thoughts?

If something comes to mind, and comes back, and comes back... in the end, it gets some connotation of reality for us. The problem is that this is often nothing real, so it creates unnecessary emotional discomfort. Fighting it intelligently is learning to identify the automatic negative thoughts that appear. This way we can later question and change them... Learn to master your thoughts to regain your well-being!

*"The work of thought resembles drilling a well: the water is cloudy at first, but then it becomes clear."*
*Chinese proverb*

## What are the automatic negative thoughts?

The reality is that our thoughts, this internal dialogue we have with ourselves, condition the way we feel and influence the way we act. Our assessment of the situation influences how we interpret it and makes us live it in one form or another on an emotional level.

Therefore, it is necessary to learn to identify automatic negative thoughts. That is, those who do not adjust to the situation and provoke very intense, lasting and/or recurring emotions about what is really happening to us.

*"There is nothing good or bad; it is human thought that makes it look like this.*

*-William Shakespeare-*

Distorted thoughts (or automatic negatives) are their own, and the content varies from subject to subject. That is, they are specific to each person. Moreover, they are discreet and spontaneous: they appear unnoticed and it is difficult to identify them as a threat when they first appear. Finally, we believe in them without being judged and generally see them as obligations (to ourselves or to others).

## Types of automatic negative thoughts

Now that we know what they are, learning to identify automatic negative thoughts requires knowing the different forms they take. The reality is that we all generate them to a greater or lesser extent. Also, as already explained, we can't control their onset, so let's work on trying to question them and change them.

For this, we have to locate them as soon as possible. It's not easy, but it's possible. The idea is to learn to balance what we think, to take perspective and to doubt if things are true. That is, we must learn to be realistic. The types of distorted thoughts we usually have are:

- Enlargement or minimization: giving excessive value to negative aspects and underestimating the importance of the positive.

- Dichotomous thinking: Classifying situations as "all or nothing," "white or black," "perfect" or "disastrous," etc., instead of seeing that in real life there are more degrees between extremes.
- Arbitrary Inference: Drawing negative conclusions without proof or contrary evidence.
- Excessive generalization: Extracting a general rule based on isolated incidents, applying the same to situations other than the original.
- Guessing thinking: thinking that others will react negatively towards us without having proof of it.
- Rigid Rules of Behavior: Feeling that we or others are obliged to do certain things. As this does not happen in reality, it usually generates a lot of discomforts (especially in our interpersonal relationships).
- Personalization: A tendency to relate things outside oneself to excessive or inappropriate involvement.

- Emotional reasoning: Believing things are this way because we feel that way.

**Example to identify automatic negative thoughts**

To understand how far the influence of these seemingly harmless thoughts goes, let's look at an example. After a meeting, a colleague tells us, "I liked how you performed at the meeting, although you seemed to be a little nervous." Maybe in the face of this situation, we might think, "Oh my gosh, I'm the worst, they'll think I'm a disaster... I always do everything wrong! I'm sure they won't want me to talk in meetings anymore. "

Here's a little bit of everything: widening the negative and minimizing the positive (we don't even notice that he liked how we present ourselves), dichotomous thinking ("I always do everything wrong", "I'm the worst" instead of seeing that there are more degrees in the middle), arbitrary inference ("I'm sure they won't want me to talk anymore"), guesswork on thinking ("they'll think I'm a disaster"), etc.

It is not easy, but if we are committed to identifying the automatic negative thoughts that appear, just as we did in the example, we will be witness to the whole process: one where we make a mountain of a grain of sand. This step is critical in learning to control our thoughts and hence our emotions.

# CHAPTER SEVENTEEN

## Strategies That Reduce Negative Thoughts

It is easy to become hostage to a dynamic of negative thoughts, especially when we have a lot of accumulation and cause inertia that mainly affects the filters we use to process information. The thoughts we speak of accumulating in the same way that small snowball increases in size when we throw it off the mountain. So an innocent little thought, released without awareness or intention, can eventually turn into a huge thing that will contaminate all our emotions, behaviors, and other thoughts.

Like the force of the ball falling unchecked, growing ever faster and faster, negative thoughts drain our energy and leave us without strength. And the more you surrender to these thoughts, the stronger they become. What's more, just as it is harder to stop that little ball after it has rolled several meters and increased in size, so is it harder to stop a ball of negative thoughts that have already started rolling.

*Thus, intervening in time to stop the ball from falling can be a good strategy and then it will not take much effort to achieve the same goal.*

## What to do with negative thoughts?

Life poses challenges for us, often without giving us any respite and without considering the resources we have. Having negative or defeatist thoughts in this scenario is reasonable. However, feeding them, keeping them, or even chasing them diminishes the quality of life and poisons our image of ourselves. What need do we have to attack our self-esteem in this way?

Negative thoughts are part of your prison, a prison that you create for yourself. Getting rid of your arrest is as simple as changing your way of thinking. Negative thinking sometimes hurts, and sometimes conditions our behaviors. It can make us act desperately when there is no need or even encourage the possibility of throwing in the towel when we still have a lot to do with our resources and our skills. Negative thoughts often condition our decisions, not exactly for good.

So why do we feed negative thinking when we know it hurts us? The problem begins when the first negative thoughts appear, and we do not handle them properly. In short, when the ball is still small and has not contaminated our whole mind. For example, some people treat the negative thoughts, or rather the anxiety they produce by "attacking" the refrigerator. A strategy that usually delivers even more negative thoughts, in this case, concerning our self-control ability and our body.

With this kind of thinking comes another curious phenomenon: Even if you are aware that you need to forget that, though, it is still challenging not to think. The more you feel you need to forget, the more present he gets. And then you ruminate on an idea that makes you uncomfortable and can seriously compromise your mental health.

## How to deal with negative thinking

So how do we eliminate these negative thoughts? In fact, negative thinking cannot be completely avoided. Sometimes these thoughts are just a spark in our mind. When this happens, we need to be aware to recognize them immediately and thus know when we are thinking negatively.

Only by being aware of our negative thoughts can we take steps to deal with them.

The following strategies will enable negative thoughts to be disabled and make the task of positive thinking easier.

1. **Observe your thinking:** Negative thoughts are usually the product of cognitive distortions or irrational thinking patterns. Watch them as if you were a bystander. If you do not let them seize your mind, they will simply disappear. Visualize them as trunks descending downstream. Sooner or later you will lose sight of them. Accept your negative thoughts and let them go.

2. **Rephrase any questions you may be wondering:** Ruminations are excessive thinking patterns. When we ruminate on an idea, we are convinced that we can solve a

situation by just thinking more about it. Something that is generally useless. You should enlighten what is really in your thoughts and discard what your mind has created before you start looking for a solution. Do not be surprised if after eliminating the fantasy you find no problem other than the ones you had created yourself.

3. **Move and work you're thinking physically:** When you are stuck in negative thinking, put it in motion. Changing the chip to arouse positive thoughts is not so easy when your mind is busy searching for a way to suffer. This is a great time to go out, take a walk, run, and dance or practice yoga. Don't stop to think - your mind is too busy - simply let your body take over and move your mind elsewhere.

4. **Avoid the triggers of negative thoughts:** a song, an image, a reading, television shows, the company of certain people... When you find out what stimuli trigger your negative

thoughts, avoid them. And, as far as possible, replace them with others that arouse pleasant feelings in you. Do not martyrize yourself or make things harder.

5. **Seek the company of positive people and pleasant experiences:** If what you see, what you hear, and what you read is positive, if the people around you are positive, it is easier to keep negative thinking at bay. Any triggers of negative thinking will be easier to eliminate if optimism is around you.

6. **Repeat statements where negative thoughts used to be:** negative thinking is often a learned habit. So, instead of allowing yourself to be invaded by any usual negative thinking, get into the habit of thinking positive under those circumstances. To remember or reinforce this attitude, you can write on paper, on your clothes, on the background of your computer or phone, or even on your own skin.

7. **Remember no one is perfect and keeps**

**moving forward:** It's easy to make mistakes, but the only thing you can do is learn from them and move on. Nothing will change however much you rumble. And if what arouses your negative thoughts is vulnerability or a limitation, focus on your strengths and your virtues. If you cannot change what exists, make the most of what you already have.

## Thoughts won't last forever

Negative thoughts are fleeting and temporary unless we encourage otherwise. They have no power of their own, but they can do a lot of damage if we give them opportunities to grow. A thought has no more power than the power you give it. Negative thoughts gain momentum when they are activated. Disabling them later is a more difficult task: it is no longer a thought, it becomes dynamic.

Each is responsible for the way they handle their

own thoughts. No matter why this thought arose: the important thing is to be able to turn it off and build an appropriate environment for these thoughts to subside. The key is to identify these negative thoughts before they have time to settle in your head and win allies.

# CHAPTER EIGHTEEN

## Beat anxiety with positive feelings

When something important is about to happen (or we want it to happen), anxiety often arises and we have in our hands what will make it bigger or smaller.

How can we put a brake on this sensation or reaction? With positive thoughts! Do not let anxiety affect your everyday life. Keep enjoying your day to day life and especially the present time. After all, as his name implies, he is a gift.

**Anxiety, the desire to travel to the future.**

If we could have a machine that would take us tomorrow, how many nerves would we save! This is true, but it is also true that we would not be enjoying anything. Of course, because the path taken is as important as the moment we reach the goal.

Let's imagine any goal (getting married, graduating,

having a child) as the destination we choose for our vacation. But by getting on the chosen means of transport to get to the place (getting married, starting school, getting pregnant), we already want to set foot on the sand, on the mountain or wherever we have decided to go.

What happens to travel by plane, train or car? We want it to pass as soon as possible (especially if it's too long). But travel is also part of the holidays.

Therefore, the organization of the party, studying to pass the tests, the growth in the child in the belly, are beautiful moments that we have to enjoy, because they will not happen again the same way. Of course we can remarry, study something else, or have a second child, but it won't be the same.

If we learned to master anxiety, every trip would be amazing and well spent. When we are anxious and nervous, it is because we have too much desire for the future, because we think that the present, today, is not important, it is just a means to reach that other destination.

In fact, happiness disappears from our lives when we constantly put it in front of our present.

I will be happy when I get married when I graduate when my baby is born. Why not be happy now as we organize the guest list, read books, or do an ultrasound? Anxiety is the unconscious mechanism we have to prevent us from something that is threatening us.

We think that what happens today is not what we are looking for and that only what will happen tomorrow is important. However, excess anxiety can evolve into a chronic disease, or rather, we can be anxious all the time for anything.

Nail biting, smoking more, getting rid of food from the fridge, not being able to sleep, having trouble concentrating at work or school, not paying attention to anything we are told, having hair loss, dark circles, tachycardia... can all be all Symptoms of an anxiety problem.

The World Health Organization (WHO) indicates that by 2020, anxiety, depression and stress will be three key factors in understanding how the disease develops. Above them, only the heart rate level and the risk of cardiovascular problems. But beware; a large part of the latter will also appear because of these three states.

Let's remember that they are not negative in themselves. The problem is when they are very intense or when they remain.

Doctors indicate that not all anxiety is bad, but we need to know how to regulate the dose. A low level of anxiety, on the other hand, is also negative for our life, because it does not allow us to focus on what we do, we have no vision for the future, we cannot plan anything, we have no goal, etc.

So how do we manage anxiety levels?

Firstly, understanding that the future, sooner or later, will come. Secondly, remembering that what we do today helps us be in this place tomorrow. The third aspect is related to taking advantage of what each day has to offer us.

Remember that nothing and no one can give you back your lost time. What good is thinking about tomorrow if you still can't enjoy today?

# CHAPTER NINETEEN
## How to Keep a Positive Attitude

For years, we have listened, read, and talked about the importance of maintaining a positive attitude to life's difficulties. But it is time to renew our thinking about it, and create new habits that will allow us to achieve what we want.

## The dangers of extreme thinking

The well-known truth is that if you let negative thoughts invade you, or if you allow depression to overwhelm you, you will go through life without realizing the good things you have. On the other hand, too much positive thinking can distort you from reality.

Excesses and extremes are not good companions. You have to change your thinking habits, your defense mechanisms against frustrations, and find the key to starting your inner motor. All of this will allow you to have a fuller life.

**Steps to Maintain a Positive Attitude**

**Identify the cause of your unhappiness.** There is always a cause for your frustration, fear, sadness or upset. It is the first thing you must do. It's not always easy but focus on finding the true cause of your frustration, which paralyzes you and doesn't allow you to reach your goal. Sometimes these are questions that go beyond what you want or can accept.

The result of this step may be pessimism. Do not be discouraged, this is just the first step towards a change in thinking habits. When facing a difficulty you can do two things: avoid it or fight it. Evading will only prolong your agony, so I recommend that you face it.

**Set a short but possible goal**. Imagine the benefits of achieving your goals. Start by creating very basic and simple habits. For example, if you want to lose weight and eat processed foods daily, decrease the frequency to just once a week and order half of what you always consume.

**The first days of change will be difficult.** Once you can do this several times, you will feel better about yourself and much more stimulated. And now is the time to set a bigger goal to achieve something even bigger, something that brings you closer to your goal and raises your level of demand.

Find out what this action is most important in truly reaching your goal. Once you have your action well defined, you can think positively and do it with as much enthusiasm as possible. This will keep you stimulated and see new possible actions. Remember that thinking positively is not effective if you do not act.

**Identify the good things you have in your life.** One of the elements that will most help you maintain a positive attitude is to thank. It is worthwhile to list everything that you consider important in your life: material goods, people, opportunities, experiences, etc.

It is common to focus so much on what we want to change that we rarely stop to see what is good about us. This is a shame because most seek to reach the next day without valuing today, and this becomes an endless race.

**Relieve your emotional burden.** As you identify the good, you will also find things and people that hurt you. It is important to think about why they are in your life; if they really hurt you, it is best to end it.

This is certainly not a simple matter. Ending relationships for years or disposing of goods that really do not satisfy you but give you a certain status is not easy. In contrast, the heavier the emotional burden, the more important the person or thing seems to be. But you will also have more freedom by letting it go.

You will be able to change your habit if, when you see what is paralyzing you, you are sincere with yourself and set possible goals, and thus find the action that leads you to overcome that obstacle and lead a more positive life.

## Positive attitude as the engine of change

Have you realized that your life is simply not what

you expected and are tired of having a negative outlook? The above advice will help you improve your life, feel happier and have a more enjoyable outlook on life by improving your everyday attitude.

## CHAPTER TWENTY
### Nine rules to achieve your dreams

As we walk down the street, we see tired, discouraged people, their faces lackluster, and quite possibly mired in sadness. However, we also see (albeit less) people with another attitude and presence; we see potential winners looking forward, confident.

Probably those in the second group are on the road to success, to their own success. But why does this distinction exist? What makes some succeed and some not? What sets them apart?

If you have a dream (we hope so, because we should all have dreams until the last of our days...), try to make it come true by following these nine rules. These are "golden rules" put into practice by those who achieve their purpose in life.

## 1. Don't make excuses

A dream is something that would fill our existence if it happened, but at the same time, it is difficult to achieve. Attention! The word difficult does not mean "impossible. " Your dreams are possible, but to reach them you must overcome obstacles and even overcome them. Do not make excuses for something possible.

## 2. Strive

In the short term it will be difficult; in the long run... you can get where you always wanted. Something difficult will require high doses of sweat, sacrifice, and commitment. Do not stop in the face of reality, strive now, reach your goal and enjoy it; or stagger between worry and frustration for the life

## 3. Never surrender

If there are obstacles, there will be times when you will need more than one combat to beat them. The effort will be immense, but successful people never surrender; that is precisely why they reached it. Do not make the path taken in vain.

## 4. Stay healthy

Although it may seem unconnected, pay close attention to your diet, sports, and medical examinations. In other words, take care of your health, as getting sick would be an obstacle that would hinder your path and further increase your waiting time.

## 5. Don't Forget Your Principles To Achieve Your Dreams

Never forget who you are. Act consistently with yourself. If you start to stray from your identity, you will not know who you are and therefore will not know why you are doing certain things. You will forget the value of your dreams... And is there anything sadder than that?

## 6. Take a risk

Achieving a dream, overcoming obstacles,

necessarily entails taking risks. The gift you already know; The risk is a mystery. So sometimes you have to choose between taking a risk and fighting for your dreams, or not taking a risk and standing still forever.

## 7. Set realistic goals

Every long-term goal implies intermediate goals. Organize the plan for your dream and see the goal by goal. In a way, this will bring you more security because, for fractions, everything will seem less risky and you will feel more control over your life.

## 8. Be Positive

Trust yourself and accept that not everything in life goes well at first. If you do not reach one of these intermediate goals now, you may be able to reach it later. Remember: If you have achieved many other things, you are capable of everything.

## 9. Sacrifice Yourself

Step by step you will arrive wherever you want. You

may have to go through great difficulties, work for low wages, not sleep for a few days. However, never forget that your dream is waiting for you and that all those sacrifices you make today will be rewarded later.

## Take control of your life

Are you hopeless and ready to give up? Your life is not what you would like? Stop for a moment, take a deep breath and remember that hardships are just challenges we must overcome. Follow these tips and take control of your life.

1- Forget all problems

When things go wrong we can't stop thinking about the problems, and that only makes the situation worse. The more we analyze, the more problems we encounter and the situation seems more difficult and stressful. Take a break and do something to distract yourself and relax. Take a walk, run, get some sleep, watch a movie, etc.

2- Analyze the situation from another perspective

Do not go around and analyze the topic from another point of view. It is important to identify the problem and change the way you act. You have the choice to continue suffering or change your attitude. In analyzing a situation, we learn a lot about ourselves, discover our fears and what they reflect. Bad times test us and shape our character.

3- Be positive

Positive thinking helps us to have a successful life. Of course, there are negative situations, but a positive attitude helps us to see the bright side of life and to thank for all we have. This is not to deny what is happening, but to find an impulse to move forward at your own pace.

4- Identify and eliminate obstacles

Discover and eliminate what makes you unhappy. Stay away from people who hurt you, destroy your credit card, stop watching TV, or anything else that bothers you. With attitude and determination, you will realize that there are several options for having more free time, saving money and doing everything that makes you happy.

5- Learn how to manage stress healthily

Stress is present in all of our lives, but anyone in control of their lives uses some effective techniques to deal with it. These people prevent stress from becoming a problem and make them lose focus. First, we have to reduce stressful situations and react with ease. Do meditation, exercise, walking, and relaxing activities.

6- Set your goals

The important thing to take control of your life is to define what you want to achieve. Without planning, we drift. Have clear goals and act as if you have already "gotten there". Little by little, your goals will begin to come true. Be persistent and true to your goals and live in coherence with your wants and needs.

Taking control of our lives may seem challenging, but it can be very rewarding. Some take control of their own life; others expect things to just happen. You have the ability to choose which path you want to walk and be happy.

# CHAPTER TWENTY ONE

## How to be emotionally strong

If, on the one hand, the emotional force can come from birth, on the other, it can also be developed from the structure of thought. All you have to do is ask a few questions, then realize your weakness or your inner strength.

Those who think weakly and fearfully will also be emotionally weak because thoughts turn into emotions.

Therefore, the formula would be as follows:

*Sad and negative thoughts = Weak emotions*

*Motivating and Positive Thoughts = Strong Emotions*

Analyze what your thinking is and you will find that it will always be in accordance with your emotions. It is very different to face a difficult situation, doubting ourselves, with fear and pessimistic thoughts, or to face that same situation with positive thoughts, such as "it will be all right", "I trust myself", "come on, you are able!", etc.

If you want to gain emotional strength, you must start thinking strongly, confidently, and positively.

Do you want to be a winner? Well, for that you should think like one.

Getting positive emotions through thinking is possible, but it takes practice and you can start to feel from the most basic emotion. To get started, just repeat a few short and motivating sentences throughout the day.

Try to spend a day without any negative thoughts invading your mind; once you get up, try to think that everything is wonderful as if you feel overwhelming security. Act and behave as you really would like to be and you will eventually become that person.

Open the curtain and think the day will be amazing, look in the mirror and say, "I love myself! I trust myself and I can get anything I want "and send yourself a kiss.

If you start the day like this, it will be like a grain of sand that will turn into a mountain. Say goodbye to pessimism, victimization, grievances, criticism and welcome security, motivation, and happiness.

How many times have we seen coaches cheering up their athletes? They give them motivation and willingness to fight, to win. They use the technique of positive motivating phrases and this often causes athletes to win the competitions.

Become your personal trainer! If you face any situation that makes you weak, think, "Let's go! Cheer up! You are capable! You are very good and you will make it! ".

## Not everything that shines is gold

Everything about phrases and positive thoughts is highly good for our mental health, but remember that if you have a problem with yourself, insecurity, shyness, etc., these things do not work miracles.

True, this can help a lot, but it acts more like a momentary soothing; it is only for those times when we are thinking positively; from the moment we stop training our mind and stop using motivating phrases, insecurity comes back with everything.

Therefore, it is most recommended that this

technique be used as a compliment, but we should always be solving the root of the problem. It is possible to buy medicine for a person suffering from anxiety... a soothing would help for a few hours, for example; but the problem will continue to exist when the effect passes.

To truly calm anxiety, it takes a professional to get to the root of the problem, whether conscious or unconscious and cut through the bad emotions that prevent a good emotional state from being achieved.

## Differences between irrational and rational thoughts

Irrational thought is defined as one that elicits very unpleasant emotional responses. These can range from anger to bitterness or terror, are long-lasting and grounded in absolutist terms (using adverbs like never or ever).

This kind of thinking is associated with what one needs to be happy, or what one should be, do, or have to be happy. That is, it has to do with self-imposed requirements. In addition, they are usually not demonstrable or verifiable thoughts.

On the other hand, rational thoughts arise as verifiable and generate emotions of much less intensity (instead of anger, discontent; rather than bitterness, resignation; rather than terror, fear).

It is important to emphasize that anger is not replaced by happiness, bitterness by satisfaction or terror by courage. Rational thinking must be realistic and coherent, and raising it in excessively positive terms can also turn it into irrational thinking.

Also, if the individual in session understands rational and alternative thoughts as positive thoughts, he or she will almost certainly not be able to propose such thoughts. A reduced state of mind and a negative-focused vision will make this task extremely exhausting.

## How can we counter emotional reasoning?

Cognitive-behavioral therapy, based on Aaron Beck's own approaches, is a good attempt to reduce this type of cognitive distortion. Here are some basic strategies you can think about:

- Identify automatic thoughts. To do this, we need to remember that our thoughts directly influence what we feel, so we must first be able to identify them and then analyze them.

- When emotional reasoning rules, feelings get mixed up with facts. Emotional thinking worsens stress, aggravates depression, and also worsens the feeling of anxiety. Therefore, whenever we experience negative emotions, it is essential to stop to reflect, analyze, channel and diminish its strength.

- Whenever you make a judgment, no matter how small, ask what emotion is behind that judgment and what mechanism led you to form this idea, this assessment.

- Ask yourself if you are able to think about the current situation in a different way. For example, if you tell yourself that you were naive to trust someone who made a mistake with you, instead of concluding that "you can't trust anyone," think that "you are no longer naive because today you have learned to lesson and surely won't make the same mistake again. "

# CONCLUSION

Positive minds are potent minds. With a mind that has the desire and dedication to doing it, we can do and accomplish virtually everything. Although this fact of life is not realized by everyone, it is probably a good attempt to allow a paradigm shift in our thinking method. You may not have realized it, but your own actions and thinking can bring about the misfortunes and tragedies in life that you are experiencing.

They tend to blame others for our own shortcomings and adversities. We believe they have contributed to our failures. Next time something goes wrong or you get any trouble, consider making a personal assessment of the situation and scrutinizing it. In some situations, our mind is influencing what we are doing and how we are reacting to people and circumstances.

Some good things can be done by a person with a positive mind. So, what do we get if we choose to think positively instead of being pessimistic?

Needless to say, in the different aspects of life, optimism brings many benefits to an individual–health, relationships, employment, satisfaction, and personal goals. Every single thought and decision that we make has an impact on our lives.

CPSIA information can be obtained
at www.ICGtesting.com
Printed in the USA
BVHW041053080321
601999BV00006B/348